A *Force for Change*

How Leadership Differs from Management

JOHN P. KOTTER

THE FREE PRESS

THE FREE PRESS
A Division of Simon & Schuster Inc.
1230 Avenue of the Americas
New York, NY 10020

Copyright © 1990 by John P. Kotter

THE FREE PRESS and colophon are trademarks
of Simon & Schuster Inc.

Manufactured in the United States of America

30 29 28 27 26 25 24 23 22

Library of Congress Cataloging-in-Publication Data

Kotter, John P.
    A force for change: how leadership differs from management / John
P. Kotter.
        p.   cm.
    Includes bibliographical references.
    ISBN 0-02-918465-7
    1. Leadership.   2. Industrial management.   I. Title.
HD57.7.K66   1990
658.4'092—dc20   89-77323
                                                                            CIP

Contents

v

Contents

IV
The Origins of Leadership

Preface

This book is the product of a research program in managerial/executive behavior which began with my doctoral dissertation on big city mayors.[1] Other parts of that program have focused on the major contextual factors that shape the way in which managers act,[2] executive careers,[3] both the organizational[4] and the power and influence[5] aspects of managerial work, the history and behavior of a group of successful general managers,[6] and corporate efforts to create a leadership capacity in their management hierarchies.[7]

This latest project began in August 1986 with questions about the nature of leadership and its relationship to management that were raised, but not answered, by my last book. The most fundamental of these questions: Is leadership really different from management and, if so, exactly how? Two phases of data gathering addressed these issues, using the usual array of methods employed throughout this program: interviews, supplemented by questionnaires, archival documents, and, to a lesser degree, observation.

Phase I was a survey designed in the summer of 1986 and conducted between October of that year and June 1987. In that study, nearly 200 senior executives in a very diverse group of twelve well-known and successful corporations either filled out a ten-page questionnaire or were interviewed at length. In either case, they were systematically asked a variety of questions about leadership and management, about people they knew who were very effective at one or both of these processes, about how well the rest of their fellow executives were handling those challenges, and about what their corporations would need from management in order to prosper over the next five to ten years.

Phase II began in June 1987 and was completed in October 1988. During this effort, a number of incidents were identified in a wide variety of settings which first-hand observers labeled "highly effective leadership in business."[8] Each of these stories was subsequently studied in some detail with the assistance of the corporations involved: American Express, ARCO, ConAgra, Digital Equipment Corporation, Kentucky Fried Chicken, Eastman Kodak, Mary Kay Cosmetics, NCR, Pepsi-Cola, Procter & Gamble, and SAS. The focus in each case study was both on facts, what specifically happened and when, as well as on opinions regarding what the facts tell us about "effective leadership." Data gathering was reasonably extensive: over a thousand pages of documents were collected, 137 interviews were conducted, individuals and their situations were observed systematically for about forty hours. (For a more detailed description of this research, see the Appendix.)

Information from these two studies was analyzed in the second half of 1988 and throughout 1989, a period in which James Leahey worked as my research assistant and was extraordinarily helpful. This analytical aspect of the project began with a search for themes in the responses to two of the questions asked in Phase I. Those inquiries were worded as such: 1) Think of someone you know personally who, in your opinion, has done an excellent job of providing his or her organization with effective management, and tell us, in as much detail as possible, what that person actually has done which constitutes "highly effective management." 2) Now think of someone you know personally who, again in your opinion, has done an excellent job of providing effective leadership to the people and activities around him or her, and tell us, in detail, what the person has done which constitutes "highly effective leadership." After completing a thematic analysis of some 200 lengthy responses to these questions, further analytical work was performed on the remaining questionnaire data. The stories from Phase II were used to test and refine the ideas that emerged from these efforts. Eventually, this manuscript was prepared.

All of this work has led me to conclude that leadership in complex organizations is an increasingly important yet often confusing topic which can be further illuminated by exploring its relationship to management, a very different sort of activity and one that is much better understood today. Such a comparison helps clarify the function, the process, the structure, and the origins of leadership. In the first chapter of this book, that comparison begins, along with the general argument that a) leadership and management are both very important processes, and the notion that leadership is "good" and management is "bad" is most certainly wrong, b) despite differences that can create conflict, the two processes can work together very successfully, and furthermore, some people can be very effective leaders and managers, and c) for a variety of reasons, many firms today lack sufficient leadership, a deficiency which is increasingly costly, yet often correctable.

In Chapter 2, the case of NCR's ATM business is presented. It is a classic example of effective leadership in business and clearly shows the essential function of leadership: to produce adaptive or useful change. The case illustrates many of the points made in Chapter 1 and implicitly raises a variety of questions which will be explored throughout the remainder of this book.

One centrally important aspect of leadership is direction setting, which people frequently confuse with planning or long-range planning. In Chapter 3, I argue that planning is a managerial process that is not the same as, nor ever a substitute for, the direction-setting aspect of leadership, a process that produces vision and strategies, not plans. Vision is defined, and the NCR situation, plus cases from American Express (its TRS business) and SAS, is used to illustrate what vision looks like in practice and how it is created.

A second core aspect of leadership is alignment: the process of getting people to understand, accept, and line up in the chosen direction. In Chapter 4, I argue that alignment is a complicated communications challenge that is very different from the design problem associated with the managerial process of organizing. How effective leadership deals with this communications problem is described and illustrated with examples from NCR, American Express, and SAS, along with the case of Kodak's copier products business.

In efforts to produce change in complex organizations, sizable barriers of some sort (political, bureaucratic, resource) are always encountered. Overcoming these barriers often takes herculean effort, which only comes from highly energized people. This is why motivation and inspiration are central aspects of leadership. In Chapter 5, we look at basic human nature to see what motivates people, and at a variety of cases (starting with Mary Kay Cosmetics and ending with an episode at Kentucky Fried Chicken) to illustrate how leadership inspires.

Many people tend to think of the structure of leadership (roles and relationships) in extremely simple terms; there is *a* leader (one role) who sets the direction, aligns followers, and motivates them. In Chapter 6, I argue that reality is more complicated, out of necessity; providing leadership on most issues in a complex organization is far too difficult and time-consuming for any one person, no matter how talented. Two cases, one at ARCO and one at Digital Equipment, are used to illustrate a variety of leadership roles.

Initiatives from people in different leadership positions do not have to converge. Instead, they can easily conflict, unless something binds them together. Traditional management coordinating mechanisms (e.g., the hierarchy, plans, job descriptions) are inadequate, at least by themselves, because of the sheer amount of non-routine coordination needed in a change effort. How thick networks of relationships fit the bill is discussed in Chapter 7 and demonstrated primarily with a case from Procter & Gamble—a story that also serves to illustrate much of the discussion from the previous six chapters.

The capacity of an individual to handle big leadership roles effectively is probably influenced by that person's early experiences. How this happens is explored in Chapter 8, the most speculative piece in the book. The limited data from this project that is applicable here is supplemented with information from two of my previous books: *The General Managers* and *The Leadership Factor*.

Adult experiences clearly influence a person's capacity to lead. The basic ways in which this happens are identified in Chapter 9, and a prototypical career of a business leader is described in some detail. This chapter also looks at how career experiences often undermine the development of leadership potential, and examines how some firms (Morgan Guaranty, Hewlett-Packard) work to systematically avoid this problem.

An organization's norms and values can encourage or limit leadership in a number of powerful ways. Chapter 10, probably the second most speculative piece in the book, discusses the case of ConAgra, where a CEO developed a corporate culture that helped create strong leadership and management both up and down the hierarchy. I conclude by arguing that the ultimate act of leadership in an organization is creating a leadership-oriented culture that continues after the creator has gone.

The book ends with a Postscript which summarizes much of the material found in all of the chapters. The reader who prefers seeing

detailed conclusions at the onset should probably examine this Postscript before starting Chapter 1.

All the cases described in this book show effective leadership. In
selecting them, I am not suggesting that we can learn only from positive examples. Cases of failed leadership can be very instructive; indeed, such stories from my previous work were used during the
analytical phase of this project. I chose not to report those ineffective
situations here simply because I think we have all seen (or read about)
far more cases of failure than of successful leadership.

Early drafts of this manuscript were critiqued by a number of indi-
viduals whose comments were most helpful. These people included:
Jerry Abarbanel, Chris Argyris, Dale Bennett, Jan Blakslee, Richard
Boyatzis, Nancy Dearman, Bob Eccles, Russ Eisenstat, Alan Frohman,
Ray Goldberg, Richard Hackman, Jim Heskett, Julie Johnson, Bob
Lambrix, Mike Lombardo, Jay Lorsch, Morgan McCall, Tom Mithen,
Charlie Newton, Barbara Rice, Vijay Sathe, Len Schlesinger, Robert
Steed, Warren Wilhelm, and Doug Yaeger. An even greater number
of people assisted me in the data-gathering phases of this project.
Most of their names are listed elsewhere in this book. My sincere
thanks goes to them all.

PART

I

Introduction

1

Management and Leadership

The word leadership is used in two very different ways in every day conversation. Sometimes it refers to a process that helps direct and mobilize people and/or their ideas; we say, for example, that Fred is providing leadership on the such and such project. At other times it refers to a group of people in formal positions where leadership, in the first sense of the word, is expected; we say that the leadership of the firm is made up of ten people, including George, Alice, etc.

In this book, I will use the word almost exclusively in the first sense. The second usage contributes greatly to the confusion surrounding this subject because it subtly suggests that everyone in a leadership position actually provides leadership.[1] This is obviously not true; some such people lead well, some lead poorly, and some do not lead at all. Since most of the people who are in positions of leadership today are called managers, the second usage also suggests that leadership and management are the same thing, or at least closely related. They are not.

Leadership is an ageless topic. That which we call management is largely the product of the last 100 years,[2] a response to one of the most significant developments of the twentieth century: the emergence of large numbers of complex organizations.[3] Modern management was invented, in a sense, to help the new railroads, steel mills, and auto companies achieve what legendary entrepreneurs created them for. Without such management, these complex enterprises

3

tended to become chaotic in ways that threatened their very existence. Good management brought a degree of order and consistency to key dimensions like the quality and profitability of products.

In the past century, literally thousands of managers, consultants, and management educators have developed and refined the processes which make up the core of modern management. These processes, summarized briefly, involve:[4]

1. Planning and budgeting—setting targets or goals for the future, typically for the next month or year; establishing detailed steps for achieving those targets, steps that might include timetables and guidelines; and then allocating resources to accomplish those plans

2. Organizing and staffing—establishing an organizational structure and set of jobs for accomplishing plan requirements, staffing the jobs with qualified individuals, communicating the plan to those people, delegating responsibility for carrying out the plan, and establishing systems to monitor implementation

3. Controlling and problem solving—monitoring results versus plan in some detail, both formally and informally, by means of reports, meetings, etc.; identifying deviations, which are usually called "problems"; and then planning and organizing to solve the problems

These processes produce a degree of consistency and order. Unfortunately, as we have witnessed all too frequently in the last half century, they can produce order on dimensions as meaningless as the size of the typeface on executive memoranda. But that was never the intent of the pioneers who invented modern management. They were trying to produce consistent results on key dimensions expected by customers, stockholders, employees, and other organizational constituencies, despite the complexity caused by large size, modern technologies, and geographic dispersion. They created management to help keep a complex organization on time and on budget. That has been, and still is, its primary function.[5]

Leadership is very different. It does not produce consistency and order, as the word itself implies; it produces movement. Throughout the ages, individuals who have been seen as leaders have created change, sometimes for the better and sometimes not.[6][7] They have done so in a variety of ways, though their actions often seem to boil down to establishing where a group of people should go, getting them lined up in that direction and committed to movement, and then energizing them to overcome the inevitable obstacles they will encounter along the way.

What constitutes good leadership has been a subject of debate for centuries. In general, we usually label leadership "good" or "effective" when it moves people to a place in which both they and those who depend upon them are genuinely better off, and when it does so without trampling on the rights of others.[8] The function implicit in this belief is *constructive or adaptive change.*

Leadership within a complex organization achieves this function through three subprocesses which, as we will see in further detail later on in this book, can briefly be described as such:[9]

1. Establishing direction—developing a vision of the future, often the distant future, along with strategies for producing the changes needed to achieve that vision
2. Aligning people—communicating the direction to those whose cooperation may be needed so as to create coalitions that understand the vision and that are committed to its achievement
3. Motivating and inspiring—keeping people moving in the right direction despite major political, bureaucratic, and resource barriers to change by appealing to very basic, but often untapped, human needs, values, and emotions

Exhibit 1.1 compares these summaries of both management and leadership within complex organizations.[10]

Management and leadership, so defined, are clearly in some ways similar. They both involve deciding what needs to be done, creating networks of people and relationships that can accomplish an agenda, and then trying to ensure that those people actually get the job done. They are both, in this sense, complete action systems; neither is simply one aspect of the other. People who think of management as being only the implementation part of leadership ignore the fact that leadership has its own implementation processes: aligning people to new directions and then inspiring them to make it happen. Similarly, people who think of leadership as only part of the implementation aspect of management (the motivational part) ignore the direction-setting aspect of leadership.

But despite some similarities, differences exist which make manage-

Exhibit 1.1 *Comparing Management and Leadership*

	Management	*Leadership*
Creating an agenda	Planning and Budgeting—establishing detailed steps and timetables for achieving needed results, and then allocating the resources necessary to make that happen	Establishing Direction—developing a vision of the future, often the distant future, and strategies for producing the changes needed to achieve that vision
Developing a human network for achieving the agenda	Organizing and Staffing—establishing some structure for accomplishing plan requirements, staffing that structure with individuals, delegating responsibility and authority for carrying out the plan, providing policies and procedures to help guide people, and creating methods or systems to monitor implementation	Aligning People—communicating the direction by words and deeds to all those whose cooperation may be needed so as to influence the creation of teams and coalitions that understand the vision and strategies, and accept their validity
Execution	Controlling and Problem Solving—monitoring results vs. plan in some detail, identifying deviations, and then planning and organizing to solve these problems	Motivating and Inspiring—energizing people to overcome major political, bureaucratic, and resource barriers to change by satisfying very basic, but often unfulfilled, human needs
Outcomes	Produces a degree of predictability and order, and has the potential of consistently producing key results expected by various stakeholders (e.g., for customers, always being on time; for stockholders, being on budget)	Produces change, often to a dramatic degree, and has the potential of producing extremely useful change (e.g., new products that customers want, new approaches to labor relations that help make a firm more competitive)

ment and leadership very distinct. The planning and budgeting processes of management tend to focus on time frames ranging from a few months to a few years, on details, on eliminating risks, and on instrumental rationality. By contrast, as shown in the chapters that follow, that part of the leadership process which establishes a direction often focuses on longer time frames, the big picture, strategies that take calculated risks, and people's values. In a similar way, organizing and staffing tend to focus on specialization, getting the right person into or trained for the right job, and compliance; while aligning people tends to focus on integration, getting the whole group lined up in the right direction, and commitment. Controlling and problem solving usually focus on containment, control, and predictability; while motivating and inspiring focus on empowerment, expansion, and creating that occasional surprise that energizes people.

But even more fundamentally, leadership and management differ in terms of their primary function. The first can produce useful change, the second can create orderly results which keep something working efficiently. This does not mean that management is never associated with change; in tandem with effective leadership, it can help produce a more orderly change process. Nor does this mean that leadership is never associated with order; to the contrary, in tandem with effective management, an effective leadership process can help produce the changes necessary to bring a chaotic situation under control. But leadership by itself never keeps an operation on time and on budget year after year. And management by itself never creates significant useful change.

Taken together, all of these differences in function and form create the potential for conflict. Strong leadership, for example, can disrupt an orderly planning system and undermine the management hierarchy, while strong management can discourage the risk taking and enthusiasm needed for leadership. Examples of such conflict have been reported many times over the years, usually between individuals who personify only one of the two sets of processes: "pure managers" fighting it out with "pure leaders."[11]

But despite this potential for conflict, the only logical conclusion one can draw from an analysis of the processes summarized in Exhibit 1.1 is that they are both needed if organizations are to prosper. To be successful, organizations not only must consistently meet their current commitments to customers, stockholders, employees, and others, they must also identify and adapt to the changing needs of these key constituencies over time. To do so, they must not only plan, budget, organize, staff, control, and problem solve in a competent, systematic, and rational manner so as to achieve the results expected on a daily basis, they also must establish, and reestablish, when necessary, an appropriate direction for the future, align people to it, and motivate employees to create change even when painful sacrifices are required.

Indeed, any combination other than strong management and strong leadership has the potential for producing highly unsatisfactory results. When both are weak or nonexistent, it is like a rudderless ship with a hole in the hull. But adding just one of the two does not necessarily make the situation much better. Strong management without much leadership can turn bureaucratic and stifling, producing order for order's sake. Strong leadership without much management can become messianic and cult-like, producing change for change's sake—even if movement is in a totally insane direction. The latter is more often found in political movements than in corporations,[12] although it does occur sometimes in relatively small, entrepreneurial businesses.[13] The former, however, is all too often seen in corporations today, especially in large and mature ones.

With more than enough management but insufficient leadership, one would logically expect to see the following: 1) a strong emphasis on shorter time frames, details, and eliminating risks, with relatively little focus on the long term, the big picture, and strategies that take calculated risks; 2) a strong focus on specialization, fitting people to jobs, and compliance to rules, without much focus on integration, alignment, and commitment; 3) a strong focus on containment, control, and predictability, with insufficient emphasis on expansion, empowerment, and inspiration. Taken together, it is logical to expect this to produce a firm that is somewhat rigid, not very innovative, and thus incapable of dealing with important changes in its market, competitive, or technological environment. Under these circumstances, one would predict that performance would deteriorate over time, although slowly if the firm is large and has a strong market position. Customers would be served less well because innovative products and lower prices from innovative manufacturing would be rare. As performance sinks, the cash squeeze would logically be felt more by investors who get meager or no returns and by employees who eventually are forced to make more sacrifices, including the ultimate sacrifice of their jobs.

This scenario should sound familiar to nearly everyone. Since 1970, literally hundreds of firms have had experiences that are consistent with it. No one can measure the overall impact of all this. But in the United States this problem has surely contributed to the fact that real wages were basically flat from 1973 to 1989, that stock prices when adjusted for inflation were less in late 1988 than in 1969, and that consumers have turned increasingly to less expensive or innovative foreign goods, leaving the country with a crippling trade deficit. And recent evidence suggests that the problem is still a long way from solved.

During 1988, senior executives in a dozen successful U.S. corporations were asked to rate all the people in their managerial hierarchies on the dimensions of both leadership and management.[14] The scale they were given ranged from "weak" to "strong", and their responses were grouped into four categories: people who are weak at providing leadership but strong at management, those who are strong at leadership but not at management, those who are relatively strong at both, and those who do not do either well. The executives were then asked if the specific mix of talent their companies had in each of these four categories was what they needed to prosper over the next five to ten years. They could respond: we have about what we need; we have too few people in this category; or we have too many people like this. A summary of their responses is shown in Exhibit 1.2.

Half of those polled reported having too many people who provide little if any management or leadership. Executives in professional service businesses such as investment banking and consulting were particularly likely to say this. The other half reported having very few people in this category, which, as one would expect, they said was just fine.

Nearly half reported having too few people who provide strong leadership but weak management. However, those who answered this way typically noted that such people were very valuable as long as they could work closely with others who were strong at management. Most of the remaining respondents reported having about the right number of people in this category for future needs, sometimes commenting that this "right number" was "very few." These respon-

Exhibit 1.2 *How Executives in a Dozen Successful U.S. Firms Rate the People in Their Managerial Hierarchies*

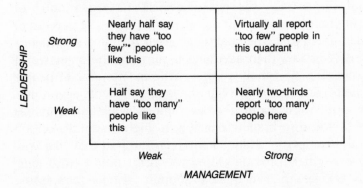

*Respondents were given three choices: (1) too few, (2) too many, (3) about right. The category having the largest number of responses is shown in the chart.

dents tended to be pessimistic about strong leaders/weak managers; they felt such people usually created more problems than they solved.

Nearly two-thirds of those surveyed said they had too many people who are strong at management but not at leadership. Some even reported having "far too many." The other third split their responses between "too few" and "about right." Those saying too few usually worked for professional service firms.

Over 95 percent reported having too few people who are strong at both leadership and management. Everyone thought they had some people like that: not super humans who provide outstanding management and excellent leadership but mortals who are moderately strong on one of the two dimensions, and strong or very strong on the other. But the respondents felt they needed more, often many more, to do well over the next decade.

This survey is interesting, not because it proves anything by itself, but because the results are so consistent with a variety of other evidence, some of which will be presented in later chapters. As a whole, the data strongly suggests that most firms today have insufficient leadership, and that many corporations are "over-managed" and "under-led."

An even larger survey conducted a few years earlier provides some insight as to why this leadership problem exists.[15] Nearly 80 percent of the 1,000 executives responding to that survey questionnaire said they felt their firms did less than a very good job of recruiting, developing, retaining, and motivating people with leadership potential (see Exhibit 1.3). These same executives also reported that their companies were not successful in this regard because of a large number of inappropriate practices (see Exhibit 1.4). For example, 82 percent of the respondents said that "the quality of career planning discussions in their firms" was less than adequate to support the objective of attracting, retaining, and motivating a sufficient number of people who could help with the leadership challenges. Seventy-seven percent said the same thing about "the developmental job opportunities available" and "the information available to high potentials on job openings in the company." Fully 93 percent indicated that "the way managers are rewarded for developing subordinates" with leadership potential was less than adequate to support the need for spotting high-potential people, identifying their development needs, and then meeting those needs. Eighty-seven percent reported the same problem with "the number and type of lateral transfers made for develop-

Exhibit 1.3 *Attracting, Developing, Retaining, and Motivating People with Leadership Potential: Results from a Questionnaire of 1,000 Executives*

I. How good a job is your company doing with respect to recruiting and hiring a sufficient number of people into the firm who have the potential some day of providing leadership in important management positions?

very good or excellent	27%
poor or fair	30%

II. How good a job is your firm doing with respect to developing these high-potential employees?

very good or excellent	19%
poor or fair	42%

III. How good a job is your company doing with respect to retaining and motivating these high-potential people?

very good or excellent	20%
poor or fair	43%

---

mental reasons across divisions." Seventy-nine percent said the same thing about "the mentoring, role modeling, and coaching provided," 75 percent about "the way feedback is given to subordinates regarding developmental progress," 69 percent about "the way responsibilities are added to the current job of high potentials for development purposes," 66 percent about "formal succession planning reviews," 65

Exhibit 1.4 *Adequacy of Practices Affecting a Firm's Leadership Capacity: Results from the Questionnaire*

The questionnaire asks 46 questions about practices that affect the firm's capacity to attract, develop, retain, and motivate sufficient leadership. In summary, people responded:

I. The vast majority of practices (80%) are more than adequate*

% answering this way=0.2

II. The vast majority of practices (80%) are adequate**

% answering this way=3.3

III. A bare majority of the practices (51%) are adequate**

% answering this way=23.7

---

*A response of 1 on a 4-point scale.
**A response of 1 or 2 on a 4-point scale.

percent about "the firm's participation in outside management training programs," and 60 percent about "the opportunities offered to
people to give them exposure to higher levels of management."[16]

Equally interesting is what was not said. Those surveyed did not say
their firms had insufficient leadership because there are not enough
people on earth with leadership potential. Instead, they put the blame
on themselves for not finding, retaining, developing, or supporting
people with such potential. Some of those surveyed readily admitted
that their firms often scared off such individuals, while others believed that they took talented young people with leadership potential
and systematically turned them into cautious managers. These rather
critical results would not be particularly surprising if they came from
a disenfranchised group of lower- or middle-level managers. But this
was not a survey of those groups. It was a poll of senior executives.

There are probably a variety of reasons why so many firms do not
appear to have the practices needed to attract, develop, retain, and
motivate enough people with leadership potential. But the most basic
reason is simply this: until recently, most organizations did not need
that many people to handle their leadership challenges.

Modern business organizations are the product of the last century.
They were created, for the most part, by strong entrepreneurial leaders[17] like Andrew Carnegie, Pierre Du Pont, and Edward Filene. As
these enterprises grew and became more complex, that which we
now call management was invented to make them function on time
and on budget. As the most successful of these enterprises became
larger, more geographically dispersed, and more technologically
complicated, especially after World War II, they demanded many
more people who could help provide that management.

A huge educational system emerged in response to this need, offering seminars, undergraduate degrees in management, and MBAs.[18]
But the favorable economic climate for U.S. businesses after World
War II allowed such a degree of stability that most firms didn't need
much leadership—until the 1970s. Then suddenly, after twenty-five
to thirty years of relatively easy growth, especially in the United
States, the business world became more competitive, more volatile,
and tougher. A combination of faster technological change, greater
international competition, market deregulation, overcapacity in capi-
tal-intensive industries, an unstable oil cartel, raiders with junk
bonds, and a demographically changing workforce all contributed to
this shift. The net result is that doing what was done yesterday, or

Exhibit 1.5 *The Relationship of Change and Complexity to the Amount of Leadership and Management Needed in a Firm*

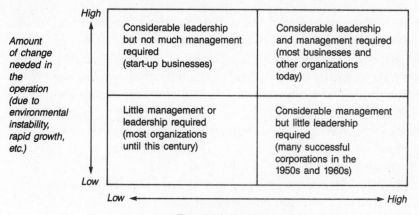

doing it 5 percent better, is no longer a formula for success. Major changes are more and more necessary to survive and compete effectively in this new environment. More change always demands more leadership (see Exhibit 1.5). But firms are having difficulty adapting their practices to this new reality.

Examples of this shift can be found nearly everywhere. Consider the case of a small- to medium-sized plant owned by a successful U.S. firm like Honeywell. In 1970, this facility employed 100 people, was 20 years old, and produced control systems for manufacturing settings. Although the facility made nearly two dozen products, one of these accounted for half the volume. That product, relatively unique in the marketplace, was protected by a number of patents. Although the plant's products were sold in over fifty countries, U.S. sales accounted for 70 percent of total volume. In the U.S. market, the plant's main product line held a 34 percent market share in its specific niche; the number two competitor controlled about 24 percent.

An examination of the demands placed on the plant manager back in 1970 reveals the following. First and foremost, he was expected to meet monthly, quarterly, and yearly targets for production, costs, and a number of other quantifiable measures. These targets were established after some negotiation by his boss and were based heavily on historical data. To meet these targets, he allocated his time over the course of the year in roughly the following way:

- 5–10%—working with his staff to produce the monthly, quarterly, and yearly plans to meet the targets
- 20–30%—working with his staff to make sure he had the appropriate organization in place to implement the plans, which in turn involved hiring, firing, performance appraisals, coaching, etc.
- 40–50%—having daily production meetings, weekly budget review meetings, and the like to spot deviations from plan as quickly as possible and to solve them
- 20–25%—all other activities, such as assisting the sales force by meeting an important customer, or deciding if a new technology should be used in one part of the manufacturing process

In other words, he spent the vast majority (75 to 80 percent) of his time *managing* the plant, with a heavy emphasis on the control aspects of management.

If a visitor to this plant in 1970 returned fifteen years later, he would have found a very different facility. In 1985, the plant had more engineers and technicians and fewer foremen and middle managers. Although the number of employees was almost the same, the output was double the 1970 levels. The plant's product line was much more volatile; products introduced within the past five years accounted for nearly 35 percent of its volume versus 15 percent in 1970. The products themselves were more technologically complex, and the technology was changing faster than it had fifteen years earlier. The plant's products were being sold in even more countries, and a greater volume was sold outside the United States. Worldwide market share for the plant's niche was about 14 percent, versus 29 percent in the United States, and its number one competitor, with nearly 22 percent of the world market, was now a Japanese company.

In this environment, the demands placed on the 1985 plant manager were in some ways similar, but in many ways different, from those found in 1970. The head of this facility in 1985 was still being asked to meet certain quantifiable targets on a monthly, quarterly, and yearly basis. That, in turn, still required producing plans, maintaining an organization, and many controlling efforts to keep things "on track." But the targets themselves were more complex and volatile due to market conditions; thus the process of achieving them was more complicated. More importantly, in addition to all these activities, there was a whole new dimension to the job, one that was time-consuming and difficult, yet essential.

In 1985, the plant manager was being asked to match his Japanese rival by finding a way to increase certain quality measures not by 1 or 5 or 10 percent, but by 100 percent. He was also asked to help the corporate manufacturing staff evaluate a number of options for moving some production out of the country, to find a way to incorporate a completely new technology into the heart of the manufacturing process, to reduce the time required to introduce new products by 50 percent, and to shrink inventories by at least a third. All of this, in turn, required much more from his staff—in terms of time, energy, creativity, and the willingness to make sacrifices and take risks. That created a huge challenge: to somehow get his people energized and committed to helping with the big cost and quality and technology issues. And all of this created change, far more than in 1970, which in turn was bumping up against a corporate bureaucracy designed for a more stable environment. It also led to the sorts of uncertainties that threatened vested interests.

The 1985 plant manager coped with these demands by allocating his time in the following way:

- 30–50%—engaging in the same types of planning, organizing, and controlling activities as did his predecessor fifteen years earlier, but using a less authoritarian style and delegating more (i.e., managing)
- 50–60%—a) trying to establish a clear sense of direction for the changes needed in quality, costs, inventories, technologies, and new product introductions, b) trying to communicate that direction to all his people and to get them to believe that the changes are necessary, and, c) finally, trying to energize and motivate his people to overcome all the bureaucratic, political, and resource barriers to change (i.e., leading)
- 0–10%—participating in other activities

By almost all standards, the plant manager's job in 1985 was more difficult than it was in 1970, primarily because the firm's business environment was more difficult. In 1985, this person not only had to manage the plant by planning, budgeting, organizing, staffing, and controlling, he also had to provide substantial leadership on dozens of critical business issues. And he was not alone in this respect.

In 1970, in a business environment that was both favorable and changing relatively slowly, sufficient leadership could be supplied by the CEO and several other people. By 1985, in a much tougher and rapidly changing environment, hundreds of individuals, both above and below the plant manager level, were also needed to provide leadership for developing and implementing new marketing programs, new approaches to financing the business, new MIS systems, new labor relations practices, and much more. Doing all this well required skills and strategies that most people did not need in the relatively benign 1950s, 1960s, and early 1970s. It required more than technical and managerial ability. Some of these people had these new skills, but many did not.

This story is interesting because the type of environmental changes involved are not at all unusual. These same kinds of changes can be found in a wide variety of industries and in a large number of countries in addition to the United States (see Exhibit 1.6).

A simple military analogy sums all this up well. A peacetime army can usually survive with good administration and management up and down the hierarchy, coupled with good leadership concentrated at the very top. A wartime army, however, needs competent leader-

Exhibit 1.6 *Results of a Poll of Mid-level Executives from 42 Countries and 31 Industries* *

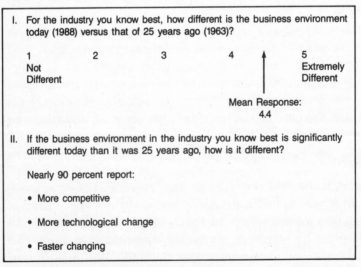

*Survey of 135 people conducted in September 1988.

ship at all levels. No one yet has figured out how to manage people effectively into battle. From 1946 into the 1970s, the world economy was, for the most part, at peace. It is no longer. But precious few corporations now have the leadership necessary to win the battles they face in this economic war.

There are a number of reasons why firms, even some very good ones, have had difficulty adapting to the new business environment. The most obvious relates to the inherent difficulty of the task. All available evidence suggests that finding people with leadership potential and then nurturing that potential is much tougher than finding people with managerial potential and then developing those skills.[19]

Experts have been of limited help, even though a few predicted the environmental changes before the fact, usually in the mid to late-1960s.[20] The biggest recommendation to evolve from this work has been a vague notion that we need to *manage* differently in the future. Individuals have stressed long-term planning, matrix structures, motivational systems and much more. As we shall see later in this book, none of the ideas have worked well, and for reasons that are predictable in light of the real difference between management and leadership.

Starting in the early 1980s some people reacted to all this by emphasizing leadership. What is needed to cope with major change, they argued correctly, is not management, but something else. Their descriptions of this "something else" were often vague. But worse yet, most suggested that this other thing—leadership—was needed instead of management. That is, they offered a prescription that was not only wrong, but dangerous.

Strong leadership with weak management is no better, and sometimes actually worse, than the reverse. In such a situation 1) an emphasis on long-term vision but little short-term planning and budgeting, plus 2) a strong group culture without much specialization, structure, and rules, plus 3) inspired people who are not inclined to use control systems and problem-solving disciplines, all conspire to create a situation that can eventually get out of control, even wildly out of control. Under such circumstances, as many small entrepreneurial firms have learned the hard way, critical deadlines, budgets, and promises can go unmet, threatening the very existence of the organization.

The most extreme, and dangerous, examples of this phenomenon are of the Jim Jones variety. In such cases, a charismatic person emerges when a group of people are experiencing considerable pain. This person is not a good manager and, in fact, does not like good managers because they are too rational and controlling. The charismatic has a flawed vision, one that does not try to create real value for both the group and its key outside constituencies. But the lack of a rational management process—that is as powerful as the leadership—means the bad vision is not publicly discussed and discredited. The strong charisma creates commitment and great motivation to move in the direction of the vision. Eventually, this movement leads to tragedy; followers trample other people and then walk off a cliff.

Seeking out, canonizing, and turning over the reigns of power to this type of charismatic non-manager is never the solution to a leadership crisis. But to move beyond this seductively dangerous prescription will require a much clearer sense of what leadership really means in complex organizations, what it looks like, and where it comes from. Given the inherent complexity of the subject matter and the barriers prohibiting rigorous empirical work on such a broad topic, satisfying such a purpose is an extraordinarily difficult task. Nevertheless, that task sets the agenda for this book, and the comparative analysis of leadership vis-à-vis the more clearly understood process of management will be the primary vehicle for achieving that agenda.

2

Leadership in Action

The story of NCR at Dundee, Scotland, is a classic example of how effective leadership coupled with competent management can produce extraordinary business successes.[1]

Dundee, a city of 160,000 people located on the River Tay about 45 miles north of Edinburgh, has roots that go back to the Roman Empire. For more than a century, the town was the most important whaling port in Britain. Later it became known for its production of jute, for fine jams from locally grown fruit, and as the headquarters of the Thompson family publishing empire.

In 1946, the National Cash Register Co. built a manufacturing plant about five miles from the town center. The 270,000-square-foot facility was opened by thirty employees recruited from its office in London. Like most of NCR's factories since the firm was founded in 1884 by John Patterson in Dayton, Ohio, the Dundee facility produced cash registers, adding machines, and mechanical accounting equipment in a relatively labor-intensive process. Products were designed in the United States and built at Dundee for the expanding European, especially U.K., market.

As NCR prospered in the strong economic climate after World War II, so did Dundee. Between 1950 and 1970, corporate revenues increased nearly one hundredfold, to $1,420,576,000. The second source manufacturing operations at Dundee grew to include nine plants by 1969. During this period the firm introduced its first computer, the National 304 Electronic Data Processing System.

In the 1970s, a new technological, economic, and competitive environment brought wrenching change both to NCR and Dundee. Technology radically altered the nature of products and production; mechanical and simple electromechanical machines disappeared, replaced by complex electromechanical and transistorized products. Technological innovation also allowed strong new competitors to emerge and challenge NCR's position in its traditional markets. A slower growing worldwide economy made matters even worse. Under the leadership of William S. Anderson, who became president of NCR in 1972, and Charles E. Exley, Jr., who became president in 1976, the firm responded by developing a new computer-based product line and by shutting down out-of-date and highly labor-intensive manufacturing facilities. Employment shrank from 100,000 to 60,000. It was a most painful period for NCR.

Dundee suffered even more so. Employment went from a peak of 6,500 in 1969 to 1,000 a decade later. Morale went down with employment levels and product quality suffered as a result. So did production; in 1979, the mostly unionized workforce walked off for nearly six weeks.

In an effort to stabilize employment levels, boost morale, make Dundee a viable operation, and take advantage of a market opportunity, management at corporate headquarters decided in late 1977 to provide the plant an opportunity associated with the automatic teller machine (ATM) business. For the first time in its thirty-year history, Dundee was given some responsibility for designing a product—specifically one aimed at that market opportunity—to replace a few thousand first-generation ATMs owned by major U.K. banks with an improved second-generation machine.

The ATM business was relatively new. It had been pioneered by a small U.S. start-up company named Docutel with a simple cash-dispensing product first introduced in 1970. Five years later the Diebold Corporation, an existing supplier to financial institutions, took the market away from Docutel by aggressively selling a much more reliable series of machines. By the late 1970s, Diebold was still the market leader in the United States. A U.K. securities firm called Chubb was number one in the United Kingdom. But worldwide, the biggest share had been captured by IBM.

Building off a first-generation NCR product designed in Dayton, the 770, people at Dundee created a second-generation product, the 1780, that was specifically aimed at replacing the Chubb machine owned by Barclays and other U.K. banks. The 1780, for example, was designed to be the same size as the Chubb product so it could fit into the same wall space. The new machines were introduced in 1979 and

Barclays ordered a few hundred of them. For a short time, the future looked brighter for Dundee. But then the first 1780s to be shipped started to break down in the field. Soon they were breaking constantly.

The problems with the ATM were related to both the design of the product and the way it was manufactured. As soon as Barclays realized the magnitude of the problem, it refused to accept delivery of any more NCR machines until the ones it had were fixed. To make this position clear to NCR, Barclays placed an order with industry leader IBM for 200 ATMs. When other NCR customers heard of Barclays' actions, they too began to refuse to accept delivery of the 1780s. And when news of this latest problem reached Dayton, Ohio, a growing number of people began to argue that Dundee be shut down, permanently.

Into this deteriorating situation, in April of 1980, stepped Jim Adamson.

Adamson, a short, intense, upbeat, youthful-looking Scot, was born on May 25, 1941, and grew up in Queensferry, a small town just north of Edinburgh and not far from Dundee. He served in the Royal Navy and then attended Heriot-Watt University in Edinburgh. From 1963 to 1973, he worked for Honeywell in its computer business. From 1973 to 1979 he held a number of jobs with ITT, including running a telephone-switching gear plant near Glasgow.

NCR first contacted Adamson in the spring of 1979. An executive search firm had identified him as someone with an excellent track record who had worked in Scotland, knew Scottish trade unions, understood electronics, and had worked in the computer industry. In a trans-Atlantic telephone call, NCR Executive Vice-President Bill Buster told Adamson they were looking for a general manager for their "problem plant" at Dundee. Adamson listened, but said he was not interested. Six months later, one of Buster's personnel managers called Adamson and asked him to a luncheon in London that included Buster himself. Adamson accepted the lunch, but nothing else. Still later came a call from NCR executive Darrell Clark with an invitation to join him in Dundee to look at the plant and then to come to Dayton to meet NCR Chairman William Anderson. Adamson accepted, and this time got hooked.

An optimistic man by nature, Adamson looked at the Dundee plant and saw a potential "gold mine." Later in Ohio, he listened with great interest as Anderson talked about his concept of "commercialization"—of taking the highly functionalized NCR structure and focusing it more on satisfying market needs by giving plants both design and profit responsibility for the product they manufactured. Although Adamson had run an engineering group and a manufacturing group, he had never had a job that included both, or a job with profit responsibility. After more communication with NCR executives, he decided he wanted the job.

Adamson began work in Dundee on April 1, 1980. He soon learned that his workforce was cynical, suspicious of management, and inclined to create work to keep themselves employed. He found a management group that sincerely did not think that the plant's problems were their fault, and who believed, for example, that their quality and costs were competitive. And he was confronted with a major crisis in the ATM area; the production line was halted because customers were refusing shipments, but incoming parts were piling up into bigger and bigger inventories.

The ATM problem received first priority. Adamson immediately stopped delivery of all incoming materials for manufacture of the 1780 and sent development engineers to customer sites to find out exactly how and why the product was breaking down. To manage what he quickly dubbed the "get well" program, he began calling meetings of his direct reports at 7:00 A.M.—two hours before work had traditionally begun for managers at the plant.

Adamson himself spent a great deal of time on the road during those first few months, talking to people at Barclays and examining the poorly performing machines. He came back from each of these trips with a long list of action items, which were then communicated at the next scheduled 7:00 A.M. meeting.

At the same time, he phoned NCR in Dayton almost daily with a summary of what was happening and submitted written reports each week. When in Dundee, he also spent a part of each day walking around the facility, getting to know people, asking questions, and listening. When he learned about specific problems, he added them to the agenda of the 7:00 A.M. meetings.

Working long hours, Adamson and his management team quickly devised an action plan for fixing the machines that were at customer sites and began to implement that plan. This basically involved redesigning the product in the field. They also put together a plan for how they would eventually restart production of the redesigned 1780s.

On July 3, three months after Adamson arrived at Dundee, Barclays felt it had seen sufficient progress in solving the ATM problem and agreed to start accepting shipments of new 1780s. Production began again. Shortly thereafter, National Westminster and Midland, two other leading U.K. banks, also agreed to accept new ATM shipments.

For three more months, Adamson worked nearly full time on the 1780 crisis: getting the machines in the field working well, producing a better product in the factory, and thus reestablishing some credibility in the eyes of key customers. To make this happen, he began to ask more aggressively for help from others at Dundee, even those beyond his direct reports. His appeal was straightforward: "We have a real crisis here that will be very tough to solve, but it is solvable. I know this is so because I have helped turn around plants before. I need your help. Either commit to work with me or get the hell out."

He also encouraged more and more honest communication at all levels about what was happening, both good and bad. He began holding monthly formal meetings with all sixty-two of his managers. He urged them to hold short meetings each week with their people, and most did. More informally, he met with small groups of people almost daily to explain what the problems were and what was being done to solve them.

As more and more people focused their efforts on the plant's key problems, results began to appear more clearly and quickly. Although he would not declare the "get well" program over for yet another twelve months, by October 1980 it was obvious to almost everyone that they were making progress on getting the situation under control.

From day one, Adamson talked "quality" to all his employees. He made it clear that he believed, from his experiences at ITT, that quality products and a high-quality plant were essential to business success. After the initial crisis was over, he began to spend more time on this simple theme. He had the plant painted and generally cleaned up. He had his management team look at all the products and production processes in the factory, not just at ATMs. He launched a quality campaign that eventually included posters around the plant, T-shirts, and even a Scottie dog—the "quality mascot."

He also began to expand contact with customers beyond discussions of the 1780 crisis, and even to expand contact beyond their current customers. In a typical visit, Adamson and one or more of his managers would meet with customers or potential customers and ask them to talk about what they would like to see in ATM products. In the second half of 1980, Adamson made nearly a dozen of these trips.

Based on some of the things he had learned from his discussions with both customers and his own employees, in late 1980, Adamson began to articulate a dream. Repeatedly he made a short speech to Dundee people, always with the same enthusiasm as if he were saying it the first time. The essence of the speech was this: "There is clearly a marketplace out there for this equipment. When we look at competitive machines, they are not nearly as good as the ideas we are developing. If we can get through this difficult period we are now in, we think we can beat the competition. This should allow us to virtually guarantee employment security. And doing all this can be fun, rewarding, and exciting. The hard part is now—to get well enough so we can buy time to turn our ideas into real products."

Not everyone bought this dream. But enough did. In 1980, the plant renegotiated its union contracts without a strike.

With this dream as a guiding force, Adamson took his development engineers, who for the most part were no longer in the field fixing 1780s, and divided them into two groups in January 1981. He asked the first to focus on developing the next generation of ATMs. He gave the second the charter of developing an intermediate product—one that would go beyond the 1780 yet be ready for sale well before the next-generation machines. In both cases, Adamson stressed that a key to new product success was "knowing the marketplace," and that both groups should spend time visiting customers and potential customers. With Adamson himself setting the pace on this issue, the engineers followed.

Then in February 1981, human tragedy was followed by economic disaster. The tragedy was the unexpected death of one of Adamson's direct reports, the director of purchasing. Instead of replacing him with an NCR employee, Adamson went outside the company and hired George Munroe, a "visionary" that he knew and respected from his ITT days. He also decided to replace his director of personnel with an outsider, Alan Murdoch. But despite the historically poor reputation of Dundee management in Dayton, Adamson chose to keep the rest of the key people he inherited. They had responded well to his leadership, and were now managing, quite competently, both the get-well program and the plant in general. Some had even risen to the challenge of helping Adamson with either the direction setting, the communication, or the motivational aspects of leadership.

The economic disaster was associated with minicomputers, a second-source product whose production runs were based on forecasts sent from Dayton. A worldwide downturn in the minicomputer market, coupled with less-than-adequate inventory control systems at the plant, left Dundee with a million dollars of inventories that had to be written off. Adamson emerged from this episode convinced that the plant needed some focus and control if it were to prosper long term, and he vowed to himself to get out of all second-source production and to concentrate on ATMs.

On March 8, 1981, Adamson sat in his office and wrote in longhand a list of eighteen questions about the ATM business, the answers to which he wanted clarified for himself and his management team. The list included: What are the key factors for success in this business? What would our customers' key factors be? Who are the major competitors? What are their strategies? Why are they more successful? What has been our strategy? Throughout the next few months he and his managers and the development engineers talked at length about these issues. By the end of 1981, those discussions, continuously enriched by additional customer visits, led to a clearer sense of where the future lay.

The vision was simple and relatively vague at first. It was of an operation that focused on the ATM business and that would become a world leader in that industry. World leadership, in turn, would be achieved by offering a wide range of superior quality products that fit customers' key needs, and by offering those products ahead of the competition.

Hard core cynics laughed at the possibility of Dundee becoming a world leader at anything. But most people were at least neutral, because they could see with their own eyes how much had changed in eighteen months.

By December 1981, it was obvious to most that Dundee was beyond the get-well stage. Sales of 1780s, especially to big customers that had been visited by Adamson and others, were nearly double 1980 levels. The plant was making money, compared to a $2.5 million loss in 1980. It was more focused; production of a number of unprofitable second-source products had been stopped. It had a growing sense of direction for future products—words like *quality* and *reliability* could be heard more often around the plant. And morale and motivation, although not high yet, were significantly above the levels found in early 1980.

Three key market needs were identified by the customer-visit program, and in the spring of 1982 the product development groups began to focus on these needs. The first was for highly reliable machines, products that were down as little as possible. The second was for products that were easy to connect to the emerging electronic banking network. The third was for products that cost a minimum, not necessarily in purchase price, but in the total costs of ownership. To introduce such products ahead of the competition, the strategy of fast-track development was created. This meant reducing the normal three-year development cycle as much as possible by, among other things, having a clear sense of direction at the onset for each design effort and eliminating unnecessary bureaucratic hurdles.

With this thinking as a guide, the design group working on the next intermediate product, the 5080, concluded that they needed a more reliable money dispenser than the one they were purchasing from an outside vendor, and that the best way to get it quickly was to help Dayton design a new one. The design group working on the first of a new generation of products, the 5070, concluded that they should create a new and more reliable software system for that machine, despite the fact that software development was officially a Dayton responsibility.

When design groups in Ohio learned of Dundee's conclusions, they resisted giving up their historical prerogatives and responsibility. People in Dayton felt that they were in a better position to make key product development judgments. They felt, for example, that the decision to create new software for the 5070 was a mistake. They also felt that their design engineers were more experienced and capable of doing actual design work, and thus that they should be solely responsible for a new money dispenser, if one were really needed.

Adamson dealt with these conflicts in different ways. Sometimes he backed away from an argument and quietly did what he wanted anyway. Sometimes he directly confronted people using market data as a shield or spear: "What customer did you get your idea from? Mine comes from talking to these 50 customers." Sometimes he appealed directly to Charles Exley, the CEO, who Adamson felt was a leader. More often than not, he got what he wanted, although it was not easy.

Getting what he wanted from his own product development group was not easy either, at least at first. In terms of the 5070, for example, Adamson concluded that customers would not be really impressed unless the reliability of his new product was twice as good as that of the closest competitor. When he first announced this at a brainstorming session with his development people, they literally laughed at him, and offered dozens of reasons why such a target was totally unrealistic. Adamson listened, but did not give in. Instead, in a scene that was to recur again and again during the next few years, he challenged them to come up with at least one reason why such a target was possible. Eventually, of course, someone did find a reason or two, and six months later, after many more meetings and a great deal of work, the head of product design, Nigel Vincent, concluded that an even higher reliability target was technically feasible. And thus "three times better than the competition" became the goal.

Work on the 5080, the intermediate product that was a direct replacement for the 1780, was completed in October 1982. The product successfully incorporated three improvements over the 1780: two better printers and a new cash dispenser. The final result stunned Dundee critics everywhere, both inside the corporation and out. Reliability was not only significantly better than that of the 1780, it was somewhat better than that of the two rival products—the 3614 and the 3624—of market leader IBM.

Buoyed by the initial success of the 5080, Dundee employees worked more energetically on the 5070, the full-function*, interior** ATM that was to be the first of a new generation of products. They wrote new software. They created or bought more reliable parts. And they designed the unit in modules that could be taken apart and put back together quickly without the expensive and cumbersome tool-kit typically needed to fix ATMs.

Adamson established an ambitious deadline for completion of the product—November 1983—so it could be introduced that December at the trade show for ATMs sponsored by the American Banking Association. His people delivered; the 5070 was ready twenty-seven days before the show.

ATM 5—the fifth such event of its kind—was held in Chicago and attended by nearly 2,500 bankers. The three-day meeting featured products from every ATM vendor in the world. Early on the first day, the people from Dundee put on a demonstration that was repeated thirty-eight more times during the course of the show. An elegantly dressed NCR employee stood on a platform with a 5070. By herself and without the aid of tools or an assistant, she proceeded to take the machine apart, placing the pieces on a nearby table, and then to put

---

*A full–function machine can do cash withdrawals, envelope deposits, account transfers, and account inquiries.

**Interior ATMs are units built for use inside a bank.

the machine back together again, all in less than fifteen minutes. At the end of each demonstration she pressed the start button, and in all thirty-nine demonstrations, the machine worked perfectly.

Most customers were clearly impressed. Dundee attendees were elated. And NCR management in Dayton, some of whom were not at all convinced that such a demo was worth the inherent risk, gave a collective sigh of relief.

Convinced they were on the right track, Adamson and his team expanded throughout 1984 most of the initiatives begun earlier. The quality program received increasing emphasis. A number of new product-development efforts were launched. The customer-visit program was broadened; Adamson himself visited customers in twenty-eight different countries around the globe that year. And a self-service product center or "branch of the future" was built right in the manufacturing area at Dundee to show off the ATM products to visiting customers.

Hundreds of customers were invited to Dundee in 1984, and nearly 190 actually came. A typical customer visit included an introductory meeting with Adamson, followed by an overview of the operation, usually presented by Ted Sims, the manager of systems program management, a discussion of quality by Neil Henderson, director of quality, a visit to the branch of the future, a demonstration of current products, and a tour of the plant. Inevitably, the plant tour guide would pause and examine a number of the quality audit charts which could be found posted quite visibly near every assembly or subassembly area, and which almost always showed that rejects/errors/problems were below targeted levels and continuing to fall.

Groups of potential customers touring the plant was but one of many signs of progress evident by mid-1984. In May, Dundee released the 5081, a full-function through-the-wall ATM. In June, orders for ATM products were strong enough that they shut down almost all non-ATM production. In July, Honeywell dropped out of the ATM business, followed shortly thereafter by a European firm named Datasaab.

Momentum continued throughout 1984 and into 1985. In May, the word reached Dundee that Docutel and Burroughs were resigning the ATM business. In June, NCR released the 5084, a cash-dispensing version of the 5080. And in July, Dundee's labor unions agreed to a three-year contract, only the second time such a multi-year agreement had been reached in the entire history of U.K. labor relations.

Adamson worked hard to get that contract. He and Alan Murdoch, his director of employee relations, met with every unionized employee, about 75 percent of the workforce, in groups of twenty or thirty. He spelled out what he thought were the advantages and disadvantages of such an agreement. He told them how he sincerely believed that this was the right thing to do. Union leaders, nevertheless, urged their members to reject the contract. When the vote was tallied, 80 percent said "yes."

The confidence that employees expressed in their management showed no signs of being misplaced. Sales of ATMs continued to grow throughout 1985. By December, orders were running at a rate ten times higher than 1980 levels. By then profitability for the plant was excellent. And best of all, preliminary figures showed that NCR was selling more ATMs than anyone in the world—more than Diebold and even more than IBM.

Adamson's success was noted in Dayton, and in January 1986, he moved to the United States to become vice-president for retail products at corporate headquarters. George Munroe was asked to run the operations at Dundee.

The year 1986 was a big one for new product introductions. In March, the 5571 and 5085 were released. The former is an interior inquiry and document printer machine, the latter a 5080 replacement with twice the reliability. In July came the 5572, an interactive video terminal developed as a sales/marketing tool, the first of a potential series of products that would go beyond the ATM business. In November NCR released the 5088, a version of the 5085 that could sit on an island at a drive-through bank.

At the ATM show that December in Los Angeles, NCR was finally able to show a full line of ATM equipment, and to do so as the acknowledged market leader; worldwide shipments in 1986 gave NCR a 35 percent share, Diebold 19 percent, and IBM 18 percent.

Market share continued to grow in the first half of 1987. In June, Dundee released the 5070L, a lower-priced model of the 5070, and welcomed back Jim Adamson as general manager. The official reason given for Adamson's return related to his wife, who refused to live in the United States, away from friends and family. Rumors circulated that there were other reasons too; some said Adamson didn't like the environment at corporate headquarters, others that Adamson's former boss, Darrell Clark, was concerned that the development programs at Dundee were losing some momentum.

Whatever the actual causes, upon returning to Dundee, Adamson

began to articulate more clearly and forcefully an even grander vision than before of what Dundee could and should become: a world
leader not just in ATMs for financial institutions but in self-service
equipment for all industries, and one of the finest manufacturing
facilities anywhere in the world, a "super plant." As before, some
chuckled or shook their heads. But the evidence continued to pour in
that, with good leadership, the Dundee people could achieve remarkable results.

By the end of 1987, statistics showed NCR's worldwide market share
for ATM shipments was up to 42 percent, its on-hand inventories
down to nineteen days (versus six months in 1980), income before
taxes up 61 percent over 1986, out-of-box audit failure down 35 percent from the previous year, and productivity up 27 percent. Return
on assets also rose 34.5 percent to a level unprecedented at NCR.

In 1988, Dundee management negotiated the second three-year
contract with its unions—the first back-to-back, multiple-year wage
agreement in U.K. history. Productivity continued to climb. So did
market share and earnings.

As Jim Adamson sat in his office in April that year describing all this
to a visitor from Boston, he took great pride in the fact that his non-
pedigreed team of Scots had been able to accomplish what far larger
and richer organizations had not; they had taken on IBM in a fair
competitive contest and beaten them. They had done so with fewer
financial resources, a less educated workforce, a geographical location that was not particularly advantageous, and a poor starting position. Their only initial source of strength was NCR's generally good
reputation with financial institutions, though credibility was deeply
strained by Dundee's first ATM product. Nevertheless, they overcame all these problems by creating a source of competitive advantage that was missing in the ATM business at IBM, Burroughs,
Honeywell, Docutel, Datasaab, and Chubb. That advantage was
strong leadership.

The precise details of how that leadership was created, of what
form it took, and of what impact it had, are idiosyncratic to this single
story. But what makes the Dundee situation interesting, for our purposes here, is that it contains so many of the themes that are usually
found in cases of effective leadership in complex organizations,
themes that will be explored in detail in the chapters that follow.[2]

These patterns relate, first and foremost, to the very process of
leadership itself (the topic of Chapters 3 to 5). Here at Dundee, as is

generally the case, a sensible vision of the future was developed along with strategies for achieving that vision—all in a process that is a lot less mystical than is often assumed. Here, as in most cases with leadership, that direction was communicated effectively to relevant parties so that they understood it and worked toward it—a communications challenge that is considerably more complicated than a managerially trained audience tends to realize. Here, as is the norm with leadership, an unusual degree of motivation was created that enabled people to overcome the difficult barriers encountered along the way—a degree of motivation that is never generated using the simplistically manipulative techniques so often described in "how to" management books. And here, as in virtually all such cases, the effective leadership was accompanied by a competent management process that operated in conjunction with it, a process that was fundamentally different from leadership, yet essential to it.

Indeed, without sound planning, structures with clear responsibilities, and good controls, the operation at Dundee may not have even survived beyond 1980; NCR's CEO told Adamson he was ready to shut the facility down in six months if the plant could not be "gotten under control," and much of what Adamson did at first was manage. But even after that, without a good management process to produce some minimally consistent results expected by Dayton, Barclays, the unions, and others, it is hard to imagine Dundee ever developing the momentum that was created after 1982, momentum that was centrally important in helping the leadership process grow and become powerful.

The basic structure of that leadership—the roles people played and their interrelationships—is also not unusual, especially compared to other small and medium-sized settings. On the surface, this structure looks extremely simple; there appears to be only one leadership role, in this case Adamson's. But an obvious clue shows that the situation is more complex; during Adamson's absence from Dundee in 1986 and 1987, the leadership process did not disappear. It may have decreased in intensity, but it continued without him. A more in-depth examination (Chapters 6 and 7) demonstrates that here, and elsewhere, there are actually multiple leadership roles held together by mechanisms uniquely suited to the function being served—mechanisms that are different from those that coordinate management roles.

At the same surface level, the origins of leadership—why Adamson was able to do what he did—are not at all obvious. This too is typical, and it usually influences us to make very simply attributions, the most common of which relates to genes; we conclude that Adamson and people like him are just born that way. Although it is not possible to say with great certainty what creates the Adamsons of this world, a more probing look (Chapters 8–10) shows it is clearly a complex product of heredity, early life experiences, important career events, as well as the culture of their current organizations. The exact patterns here are especially important because of their implications for action—for increasing the amount of effective leadership in organizations.

Perhaps most clearly of all, the Dundee story shows the most common function of effective leadership in modern complex organizations: to produce change, often dramatic change, in some useful direction. The Dundee organization in 1988 was very different from its predecessor in 1980. Almost all of the people involved in the story, from shop-floor workers to Dayton executives to customers at Barclays, would agree that the overall change was unquestionably for the better. It gave a variety of different groups of people something of real value. Employees received job security, many more promotion opportunities, and huge increases in self-esteem from a job well done. Customers got a set of products that more closely met their real needs. Suppliers received additional business. Dayton got a gigantic increase in net income and far fewer headaches. Even shareholders of the parent corporation received a somewhat better stock price because of Dundee's profitability.

But as dramatic as these results are, they are not unusual in cases of effective leadership.[3] Indeed, the promise of major change for the better is at the very heart of what leadership is all about. It always has been. The great political, military, and religious figures from history have undoubtedly understood this well. Today it is increasingly important that managers do also.

PART

II

The Process of Leadership

3

Establishing Direction

Leadership produces change. That is its primary function. In cases of effective leadership, the direction of that change is carefully selected in an activity that is at the core of what leadership is all about. To understand that activity, it is absolutely essential to recognize what it is not. Setting direction is never the same as planning or long-term planning, although people regularly confuse the two. Planning is a management process, fundamentally deductive in nature, and primarily designed to help produce orderly results, not change. That is quite different from the direction-setting aspect of leadership.

Knowing that the sales force has promised an important customer that a certain amount of one of their products will be delivered on, for example, May 1, the plant's management puts together a "plan" to help ensure the promise is kept. The thought process of creating that plan starts with the desired target and then works backwards in time, deducing what will be necessary to meet that goal. Thus, deduction number one: To have that order delivered on May 1, transportation people need to arrange for shipping on or about April 24. Deduction number two: To ship on April 24, final assembly will need to complete the order during the first three weeks in April. Deduction number three: Because the current assembly plan doesn't have that much spare capacity, people will have to be added to the third shift. Deduction number four: To have the right parts ready for assembly during April, parts manufacturing will need to . . . . Deduction number five: For this to happen, purchasing will have to . . . . And so on and so forth.[1]

35

The output of this type of exercise is typically a statement of every-thing that needs to be done between the present and the target date. It might also include a budget—budgeting being a planning process for achieving fiscal targets. If the final statement is long and compli-cated, and thus hard to remember and communicate, it will usually be put in writing. Otherwise, it will be committed to memory and passed along to others verbally.

Plans are typically given or communicated to all the relevant people in the organizational structure so that individuals know what is ex-pected (e.g., the purchasing agent knows what he must do by January 15). They are also used as part of the control process; by regularly comparing plans to actual events, managers can quickly spot and cor-rect problems.

Good planning of this nature is incredibly important in organiza-tions today. Businesses are so complicated because of the number of people involved and the interdependence of activities that, without good planning, commitments to customers, employees, or stockhold-ers would often go unmet, with all the inherent problems that tend to follow. Without it, organizations have a tendency to lurch from one crisis to the next, exhausting people, resources, and money in the process.

But even the very best planning possible is not the same as leader-ship—or, more precisely, the direction-setting aspect of leadership. Nor is it a replacement or substitute for leadership.

The direction-setting aspect of leadership does not produce plans; it creates vision[2] and strategies. In the sense that it is used here, vision is not mystical or intangible, but means simply a description of some-thing (an organization, a corporate culture, a business, a technology, an activity) in the future, often the distant future, in terms of the essence of what it should become. Typically a vision is specific enough to provide real guidance to people, yet vague enough to en-courage initiative and to remain relevant under a variety of condi-tions. Visions can be good or bad. We usually think of them as good (or appropriate) if they pass both desirability and feasibility tests.[3] Desirability is defined in terms of how well the future state described in a vision serves the interests of important constituencies— customers, stockholders, employees. Feasibility is demonstrated by a strategy, often a competitive strategy, that explains how it is realisti-cally possible, although not guaranteed, to eventually achieve the de-sirable state. Conversely, bad visions tend to ignore the legitimate needs and rights of important constituencies and/or to be strategi-cally unsound.

For example, the direction that evolved in 1982 at NCR Dundee might be summarized as such: The future lies in the ATM business, with Dundee becoming the industry leader. Seeking, and then achieving, world leadership in ATMs is desirable because it should bring with it a level of profitability and growth that will meet or exceed the highest expectations of NCR management in Dayton and allow job security, wages, and promotional opportunities that meet or exceed the hopes of Dundee employees. Such a goal should be strategically feasible by offering a product line that meets customers' most important needs, and doing so ahead of the competition. That, in turn, should be achievable by means of a combination of Dundee's company-visit and fast-track development programs, neither of which is being pursued aggressively by any competitor. Such a strategy should create a defendable advantage, because once it begins to work, competitors will have great difficulty catching up, due to the nature of fast-track development.

Direction of this kind is usually produced by a process that is largely inductive in its analytical approach. That is, it gathers a broad range of data on the context and looks for patterns, relationships, and linkages that help explain things. It is driven by the sorts of questions that Jim Adamson of NCR Dundee raised: Who are our competitors and why are some succeeding more than others? Why are some succeeding more than us? Who are our customers and what helps them to succeed? How is all this changing? In this environment, what are our major strengths? What are our most important weaknesses? Rarely are these questions answered by a single individual. Many people become involved, out of necessity. Frequently, however, they are challenged to do so by one person, like Adamson, who sets the pace by raising issues and listening carefully to responses.

This direction-setting process tends to continue over time, once started, although it will usually go through periods of both great activity and very little activity. As such, visions and strategies tend to be dynamic, not static, and evolve. The direction at Dundee, for example, was somewhat different in 1981, 1983, and 1987.

The output of this activity is usually much more compact than a plan; although less likely to be written down, visions and strategies can usually be stated on a few pages. They are much less likely to be numerical in nature than a plan. And unlike plans which seek to eliminate risks, visions and strategies always have some degree of uncertainty built into them out of necessity; it simply is not possible to make major change without undertaking some risk.

Neither plans nor visions and strategies are substitutes for one another because they serve different purposes. The former helps people get things done consistently and predictably, whether that is doing what has been done before or trying to move in a new direction. The latter helps produce change, in products, marketing, finances, or even in the way a firm manages itself (see Exhibit 3.1).

A lack of recognition of these distinctions has caused more than a few over-managed and under-led corporations to embrace "long-term planning" as a panacea for their lack of direction and consequent inability to adapt to an increasingly competitive and dynamic business environment. Such an approach cannot work, and for reasons that are relatively easy to see once one appreciates the difference between planning and direction setting.

First of all, long-term planning, because of the scope of the activity, is always time-consuming. Yet whenever something unexpected happens, plans have to be redone. In a dynamic business environment, the unexpected often becomes the norm, and long-term planning thus becomes an extraordinarily burdensome activity. This is why most successful corporations limit the time frame of their planning

Exhibit 3.1 *Creating an Agenda: Management vs. Leadership*

	Management: Planning and Budgeting	Leadership: Establishing Direction
The primary function	To help produce predictable results on important dimensions (e.g., being on time and on budget) by planning for those results	To help produce changes needed to cope with a changing business environment (e.g., new products, new approaches to labor relations) by establishing a direction for change
A brief description of the activity	Developing a plan: a detailed map, put in written form if it is complicated and hard to remember or communicate, of how to achieve the results currently expected by important constituencies like customers and shareholders, along with timetables of what must be done when, by whom, and with the costs involved; doing so by means of a deductive process which starts with the needed results and then identifies the necessary steps, timetables, and costs	Developing direction: a vision which describes key aspects of an organization or activity in the future, along with a strategy for achieving that future state; doing so by means of an inductive process of gathering a broad range of information about the business, organization, or activity, answering basic questions about that domain, testing alternative directions against that understanding, possibly experimenting with some of the options, and then choosing one

activities, and why some even consider "long-term planning" an oxy-moron.

But in a firm without direction, even short-term planning can be-come a management black hole, capable of absorbing an infinite amount of time and energy. With no vision and strategy to provide constraints around the planning process or to guide it, every eventu-ality deserves a plan. Under these circumstances, contingency plan-ning can literally go on forever, draining time and attention from far more essential activities, yet without ever providing the clear sense of direction that firms so desperately need nowadays. After a while, managers inevitably become cynical about all this, and the planning process can degenerate into a highly politicized game.

Planning works best not as a substitute for direction setting but as an activity that is complementary to it. That is, a competent planning process serves as a useful reality check on direction-setting activities. It can answer questions like: Is it possible to take the first few steps needed to get there from here? Can we really afford to do this? Like-wise, a competent direction-setting process provides a focus in which planning can then realistically be carried out; it clarifies what plan-ning must be done and what planning is irrelevant (see Exhibit 3.2).

Organizations that are both well led and well managed understand all this. But they are in the minority today.

Exhibit 3.2 *The Interrelationship of Direction Setting and Planning in a Complex Organization*

The direction-setting process creates

- Vision—the kind of organization people aspire to create in the long term— 3–20 years

- Strategies for achieving the vision— 1–5 years

Provides focus

Provides a reality check

The planning process creates

- Formal/written plans—6 months to 2 years
- Unwritten plans—1 day to 1 year

A good example of effective direction setting can be seen in the Travel Related Services (TRS) arm of American Express during the years from 1978 to 1987.[4] This is a case that is contextually very different from NCR's: service versus manufacturing, a U.S. base versus European, large scale versus moderately small, a mature business versus a young one, and a successful situation versus a turnaround candidate. Yet as in the NCR case, the development and use of visions and strategies is directly related to an organization's outstanding performance.

TRS, the historical core of American Express, has roots that go back to the firm's founding in 1850. Its first big product was a money order aimed at thwarting the robberies of Jesse James. By the 1970s, the money order had long been replaced in popularity by traveler's checks and the American Express card. These and related services were very successful, but TRS was facing problems often associated with increasing competition in a mature business.

By 1978, hundreds of banks were either offering or planning to introduce their own credit cards through Visa and MasterCard. More than two dozen financial service firms were also entering the traveler's check business. A *Fortune* article written that year predicted that TRS "will find it progressively harder to keep the glow on profits."[5] This was a logical conclusion, because more intense competition, in a mature market place, should reduce margins and prohibit growth.

At the center of this story is Lou Gerstner. A cherubic-looking Dartmouth graduate with a Harvard MBA, Gerstner worked at McKinsey for thirteen years before accepting the invitation of AmEx's new chairman, Jim Robinson, to join TRS in 1978 as an executive vice-president. He then became president of TRS in 1979.

Gerstner began his job at American Express with ideas that were developed while he was at McKinsey. As a consultant to TRS for nearly five years, he had spent literally thousands of hours focusing on the money-losing travel division and the increasingly competitive card business. The process was pure McKinsey, at which Gerstner had become most highly skilled. It began by asking fundamental questions about the economics, the market, and the competition. It involved the use of a team of seven or eight people to gather a broad range of data to address those questions. It stressed thinking hard until a deep understanding of that business was thoroughly developed.

At TRS, Gerstner shocked the people running the card organization by bringing them together within a week of his appointment as their new boss and then proceeding to question all of the principles by which they conducted their business. He did so by asking the most basic of questions: How do customers view our products and services? What is our position against our competition? What are our key economic levers? In particular, he challenged repeatedly two widely shared beliefs—that their product was mature, and thus limited in potential for both growth and innovation, and that they should have only one product, the green card. Over the following year, he set up dozens of additional strategy meetings to talk about these issues. He also converted to this use an equal number of sessions officially scheduled for other purposes.

At all these meetings, he showed little tolerance for formal "dog-and-pony" presentations. Instead he demanded real discussions, with a focus on facts and on "hard nosed, analytical, strategical, competitive thinking." In his second year at American Express, he took the same approach toward the traveler's check business. Still later, all the businesses became involved.

Through this kind of a process, a vision began to develop of a TRS that looked nothing like a 130-year-old company in a mature industry. The vision was of a dynamic and growing enterprise that was economically prosperous despite the onslaught of Visa and MasterCard competition from thousands of banks. The strategy for achieving this vision was multi-layered, and varied somewhat from product line to product line. In general, it first called for an almost obsessive focus on the marketplace globally, and specifically on the kind of relatively affluent customer American Express had been traditionally serving with top-of-the-line products. It called for further segmentation of this market, and then the aggressive development and marketing of a broad range of products/services tailored to appeal to each segment. When combined with an emphasis on investing intelligently to continuously increase productivity (and thus lower costs), TRS people felt that this approach could provide the best customer service possible (better than Visa and MasterCard could ever provide) to a market that had enough discretionary income to buy many more services from TRS than they were then buying (and thus the great growth potential).

To achieve all this, the next strategic layer called for the development of a more entrepreneurial culture, the hiring and training of an outstanding group of dedicated people who would thrive in that culture, and the clear communication to them of the overall direction.

These kinds of people, in the entrepreneurial culture, with a clear sense of what they were trying to achieve, would then make the first layer of the strategy a reality. Furthermore, said TRS executives, none of our competitors are in a good position to copy this because they, particularly banks, will find it much harder to be enterpreneurial and to attract the very best employees.

As soon as this sense of direction began to take shape, it was communicated to relevant parties throughout TRS. Gerstner led the way in trying to make it happen. Eventually, more and more people bought into this ideal and became excited about pursuing it.

As a result, a more entrepreneurial culture was developed. At first Gerstner, then other top managers, tried to encourage intelligent risk taking, and when it happened, did everything possible to reward it. Gerstner made himself the head role model, amazing people at first with what seemed to them radical decisions. To revitalize the money-losing and low-status travel division, for example, he took the corporate card out of the card division and gave it to travel along with some of the card's best executives.

To make entrepreneurship easier, TRS management began to discourage unnecessary bureaucracy—procedures and paperwork, for example, that served little purpose. Gerstner made a personal crusade of cutting down the number of useless memos.

Hiring standards were upgraded. Gerstner talked constantly about "quality" people. He sent his recruiters to the best schools and asked them to recruit the best students. To attract good people and help them to grow, he created the TRS Graduate Management Program. This initiative offered high potential young people special training, an enriched set of experiences, and an unusual degree of exposure to top management.

Again and again, the new direction was communicated until both bright young people and senior TRS employees really did focus on the TRS marketplace through the eyes of that vision. And when quality people in an entrepreneurial culture did so within a context that included sufficient basic management discipline (also stressed by Gerstner), new products/services/initiatives began to emerge that were received well in that marketplace.

In 1978, TRS began to expand its overseas presence dramatically. By 1988, AmEx cards were issued in twenty-nine currencies versus eleven a decade earlier. In 1979, the firm began to focus aggressively on two other market segments that had historically received little attention: women and college students. In 1981, TRS combined its card and travel-service capabilities to offer corporate clients a unified system to monitor and control travel expenses. Direct marketing, selling merchandise through the mail, had been a part of American Express since 1967. But during the early 1980s the number of goods offered to customers was greatly increased, and by 1988, AmEx had grown to become the fifth largest direct mail merchant in the United States.

The concept of cause-related marketing was first tried in 1981, most visibly attached to the 1983 Statue of Liberty Restoration, where money is donated to a cause by American Express for every new card member and every card, traveler's check, and travel transaction. During the Statue of Liberty campaign, card use rose by 28 percent and new membership by 45 percent. The Platinum card was also introduced in 1984, and *Fortune* magazine named it one of the best new products of the year. In 1987, the regular card was enhanced with "Buyers Assurance," which offers insurance for 90 days on all purchases made with the AmEx card. Shortly after its introduction, merchandise bought with the card increased 28 percent. Also in 1987, a so-called revolving credit card was introduced. Named Optima, it was honored by *Fortune* as one of the best new products of 1987. In 1988, the firm switched to image-processing technology for billing, producing a more convenient monthly statement for customers and reducing billing costs by 25 percent.

Within a context that was also well managed, all of these leadership successes translated into a steady growth of revenues and profits that defied the laws of a mature marketplace. Between 1978 and 1987, TRS's net income increased a phenomenal 500 percent, about 18 percent per year compounded. It literally out-performed many so-called high-tech/high-growth companies. With a 1988 return on equity of 28 percent, it also out-performed most low-growth but high-profit businesses. And it did all this despite the predicted onslaught of competition.

Overall, not a bad performance for a 130-year-old company.

Discussions of vision and its development have a tendency to degenerate into the metaphysical. The implication is that this is really very mysterious and certainly not something in which mortal human beings, even very talented ones, should engage. Stories like the one at TRS show that this all-too-frequent conclusion is simply not true. The development of good business direction is not an act of magic. It is mostly a tough, sometimes exhausting, information-gathering and analytical process. People who help develop such visions and strategies are not magicians. They tend to be broad-based strategic thinkers who are willing to take risks. An effective business vision itself is not cloud-like. It can be defined quite clearly in its form and function (as in Exhibit 3.1).

Furthermore, although visions and strategies are sometimes brilliantly innovative, in a sort of magical sense, most of the time they are not. Business visions regularly have an almost mundane quality to them. They are usually made up of ideas that are well known. Often the exact combination or patterning of the ideas is new. But sometimes even the overall directional pattern—desired future states, logic as to why they are desirable, strategies for getting there, logic as to why strategies are feasible—is not new. But it works, nevertheless, either because the competition has no sense of direction, is pursuing a bad vision, or has similar strategies which they cannot get their people to embrace.

The case of Scandinavian Airline Systems (SAS) is instructive in this regard.[6] Like most firms in its highly regulated industry, SAS did well in the economic boom that followed European recovery from World War II. For sixteen straight years, starting in 1962, it made money every year. In 1978 it saw record profitability. But in 1979, the year in which airlines were deregulated in the United States, and six years after the first oil shock, the industry was beginning to change everywhere, and SAS started to suffer losses. When Jan Carlzon took over as COO in 1980, the firm was headed toward a $20 million deficit, a very large figure for a firm its size.

Carlzon, a handsome and charming Scandinavian, has spent his entire career in the travel industry. He started at Vingresor, a subsidiary of SAS that assembled and sold vacation package tours. In 1978, he went on to become President of Linjeflyg, Sweden's domestic airline and an affiliate of SAS. Then he became COO of SAS in 1980, and CEO a year later.

As head of SAS, Carlzon quickly decided that the firm needed a "new course." To make this happen, he appointed a seasoned team of executives to handle every day management of the firm. Then he and a group that he assembled concentrated on developing a new direction and communicating it to SAS's work force, its board of directors, its unions, and relevant aviation authorities.

The vision which emerged was basically this: SAS will strive to become known as the best airline in the world of the frequent business traveler. This is a desirable objective because, if attained, it will offer

high enough margins (business passengers tend not to shop for dis-
counted fares), steady enough business (the corporate market flies
during good times and bad, and keeping expensive planes full is important), and enough growth potential (there are a lot of business
travelers in the world and SAS has only a small market share) to
satisfy all relevant constituencies. To achieve this objective, SAS will
pursue a strategy that focuses capital expenditures and management
time on satisfying those few things that business travelers really care
about, such as punctuality and frequent flights between business cen-
ters, while not spending money or time elsewhere.

The point of this vision was not to reject either a cost-conscious or
rich vacation traveler. To the contrary, SAS would be happy to serve
both. But it would not spend time or money trying to satisfy the idiosyncratic needs of those secondary markets. Dozens of other airlines
could do so. If, for example, Airbus, McDonnell Douglas, or Boeing
offered a new airplane that was a technological wonder, was loved by
vacationing travelers, but was not necessary to serve this business
market, then they simply would not buy the plane. Period.

The central idea in this vision, regarding the advantage of the business frequent flyer, was anything but original. The entire industry
knew that business travelers were willing to pay higher fares and
flew more consistently. They also all knew that different market segments had different concerns, and thus one could spend money to
satisfy segment A and get nothing at all for segment B except, perhaps, higher prices to pay for the increased costs. But in an industry
that was known more for bureaucracy than vision, no one had ever
put these simple ideas together and dedicated themselves to moving
in the direction so implied. SAS did, and it worked.

By 1982, the airline was profitable once again and growing, despite
an overall loss that year of $2 billion for international airlines world-
wide. By 1983, net income, customer satisfaction, and employee morale had risen to the point that *Air Transport World* named SAS
Airline of the Year. At least one other magazine named it the best
airline in the world for business travelers. Profits continued to grow
at a phenomenal rate, and in 1988, reached $600 million, over twenty-
five times higher than the best pre-Carlzon year (1978). The mundane
vision had become a reality, and with it came both fame and fortune.

Adamson and his team wanted to be number one in ATMs in the
world. Gerstner, et al., wanted to offer better customer service to
their TRS market than anyone else in the world. Carlzon wanted SAS

to become known as the best airline in the world for the frequent
business traveler. Lee Iacocca, when he took over an ailing Chrysler
Corporation, talked of "just wanting to be the best."

The notion of wanting to be the best at something is a far more
common theme in successful business visions than most people realize. One finds it in small and large situations, in high-tech and low, in
the United States and abroad. In successful cases, the "best" theme is
never alone, in the sense of simple bravado. It is always connected to
a sensible strategy or set of strategies. But again and again, it is there.

Sir John Harvey-Jones is widely credited for having provided excellent leadership that helped transform Britain's ICI from a lumbering
giant into a profitable competitor in the chemicals industry.[7] He be-
lieves, and many would agree with him, that there are several reasons why we find this "best" theme as often as we do. Says
Harvey-Jones: "The aim of the business leader must be to be the best,
for only the best command their own destiny and achieve the sort of
rewards that are sought for themselves and their people. In a cycle of
reinforcement, the best people wish to join the best companies. The
best companies are able more readily to make alliances or purchase
technology or be welcomed into countries other than their own, or
obtain financial consideration from banks or shareholders, or escape
some of the more scathing criticisms which can be so damaging to a
company if produced in the public arena."[8] In other words, being the
best at something can offer a variety of significant rewards which
make such a state of affairs very desirable, and which, in total, can be
a powerful source of competitive advantage. This insight may appear
obvious. Yet the world today is full of organizations that seem to be
quite content at being second or fifth or tenth best at some activity.

The directions pursued by NCR, TRS, and SAS have one additional
element in common that is also worth noting. In all three cases, their
strategies for becoming the best at something included a strong reference to developing a less bureaucratic and more entrepreneurial environment. The exact words they use vary, but the ideas are very
similar. The implicit logic here has considerable face validity; in an
increasingly competitive global marketplace, it is hard to imagine
slow and cumbersome bureaucratic organizations becoming the best
at anything. Again, this seems so obvious. But the world today is full
of highly bureaucratic organizations, some of which have no clear
direction (see summary of direction setting in Exhibit 3.3), and are
doing remarkably little to change that state of affairs. That's what
happens when firms are "over-managed" and "under-led."

Exhibit 3.3 *Establishing Direction*

Direction	A description of something in the future (a vision), often the distant future, and a strategy for getting there. A good vision satisfies two tests: desirability and feasibility. Desirability means the needs of the constituencies that support the business or organization (e.g., customers, shareholders, employees) are met. Feasibility means there is a sensible strategy for getting there, one that takes into account the competition, the organization's strengths and weaknesses, technological trends, etc. A firm's direction can be very novel but often is not.
Creating direction	Gathering a broad range of information about an activity or business, especially from customers. Challenging conventional wisdom and analytically looking for patterns that answer very basic questions about that activity or business (e.g., what is required to succeed in the business? How do customers view our products/services?). Generating and then testing alternative directions against this understanding. Possibly even experimenting with some options. Finally choosing a good one (i.e., one that is both desirable and feasible). Doing all this in a dynamic way that never really ends (although the process can go through periods of great activity and periods of relative inactivity).
Potential impact	Clear direction helps produce useful change, especially significant or non-incremental change, by pointing out where a group should move, by showing how it can get there, and by providing a message that is potentially motivating/uplifting.

4

Aligning People

A central feature of modern organizations is interdependence, where no one has complete autonomy, and most employees are tied to many others by their work, technology, management systems, and hierarchy. These linkages present a special challenge when organizations attempt to change, and thus to the process of leadership; unless a large number of individuals line up and move together in the same direction, people will tend to fall all over one another.

To an audience that has been overeducated on management and undereducated in leadership, the idea of getting people moving in the same direction appears to be an organizational problem. It is not. Organizing is a managerial process with a different function and character. The relevant activity here is called aligning.

Managers "organize" to create human systems that can implement plans as precisely and efficiently as possible. Typically, this requires a number of potentially complex decisions. A structure of jobs and reporting relationships must be chosen from among an infinite number of possibilities. That structure must be staffed with individuals, which in turn requires matching people and jobs. If the people do not have all the skills and knowledge needed to do their jobs, not an unusual situation, decisions must be made regarding what training or coaching to provide. Plans always need to be communicated to employees, and then still more decisions must be made regarding exactly how much to delegate and to whom. Economic incentives usually need to be constructed to encourage plan accomplishment, and again, there are always many alternatives. The same can be said about systems for monitoring plan implementation.

These organizational judgments are, in many ways, much like architectural decisions. The essence of the issue is a question of fit within a particular context. Does the structure fit the tasks inherent in the overall plan? Does this person fit that job? Does this compensation package fit the goals of the plan and the type of people involved? In the last twenty years, we have come a long way in making a science, of sorts, to answer these questions.[1] But just as architecture is a blend of art and science, organizing still must rely on a lot of difficult judgments.

Aligning is different in at least three fundamental ways, all of which combine to make it more of a communications challenge than a design problem.

Although organizing can mean talking to many individuals, it almost always involves fewer than are potentially relevant in a leadership effort. Sometimes far fewer people. In Jim Adamson's case, the maximum number of jobs that he could have tried to organize in 1982 was around 1,000, the total employment at NCR Dundee. But at that same time, the number of people who needed to be aligned to his emerging direction, if one included his own employees, people in Ohio, key customers, and essential suppliers, was at least twice as many, perhaps more.

Adamson's situation was not unusual. When attempting to communicate with people in an alignment effort, the target population can involve not only those that report to a specific management job, but also bosses, peers, staff in other parts of the organization, suppliers, governmental officials, or even customers.[2] Indeed, anyone needed to help implement the vision and strategies or anyone in a position to block implementation can be relevant.

The communication to the target population in an organizational effort can certainly be complicated. In a complex business, helping people to understand the latest plan and their role in it is no small chore. But trying to get people to comprehend a vision of a very different future is a communications challenge of a totally different magnitude.

Much of this has to do with the difference between routine and non-routine, between doing something that has been done before versus doing something new. The former usually requires less communication than the latter, is typically more easily understood, and is more readily accepted as credible. It is much like the difference be-

tween a quarterback in football attempting to tell his team the next
two or three plays versus his trying to explain to them a totally new
approach to the game to be used in the second-half of the season.
Giving out three plays can literally be done in a dozen words, with the
chances of effective communication extremely high. The probability
that the message will be seen as legitimate and credible is also very
high. Almost the opposite is true in the second case: that of explaining
a new competitive philosophy. Many more words are needed; one
can imagine someone going on for hours. The words quite probably
will not be understood by everyone. Even if they are understood,
they may be rejected by those who question whether the team really
needs a new philosophy or whether the quarterback is a credible
football philosopher.

Delivering a complex message to a large, diverse, and skeptical audience can be incredibly difficult, especially in big or geographically
dispersed organizations. No less a luminary than Jack Welch, chairman of GE, has candidly admitted that: "Without question, communicating the vision, and the atmosphere around the vision, has been,
and is continuing to be, by far the toughest job we face."[3]

The point is not that aligning is simply more difficult than organizing, although it always is on the communications dimension. The critical point is that they are different (see Exhibit 4.1), and if one does
not recognize the differences, predictable problems arise.

Consider, for a moment, what would most likely happen if someone
approached aligning with an organizing mentality. Such a person
would probably focus almost entirely on his own employees, perhaps
only on those that report directly to him. He would probably under-
communicate, not by a little, but by a lot. He would probably do few
things to expand the credibility of the message or the messenger; the
tone would be "I'm the boss and here are the marching orders." And,
as a consequence of all this, he would probably fail to get his needed
alignment by a significant margin. One can only speculate how often
this scenario has actually occurred. It certainly is not rare.[4]

One of the most visible characteristics of a successful alignment process is what appears to be a great deal of communication. In an abso-
lute sense, the amount of information transmitted is probably not
large compared to what is typically communicated as part of the control aspect of management. But to an audience who has been taught
to hand out marching orders with short commands, it certainly can
seem to be an extraordinary amount of conversation.

Exhibit 4.1 *Developing a Human System/Network for Achieving Some Agenda: Management vs. Leadership*

	Management: Organizing & Staffing	Leadership: Aligning People
Primary function	Creating an organization that can implement plans, and thus help produce predictable results on important dimensions (e.g., costs, delivery schedules, product quality)	Getting people lined up behind a vision and set of strategies so as to help produce the change needed to cope with a changing environment (e.g., new products, new approaches to labor relations)
A brief description of the activity	A process of organizational design involving judgments about fit: what structure best fits the plan, what individual best fits each job in the structure, what part of the plan fits each person and thus should be delegated to him or her, what compensation system best fits the plan and the people involved, etc.	A major communications challenge: getting people to understand and believe the vision and strategies by communicating a great deal to all of the individuals whose cooperation or compliance may be needed to make that direction a reality, and doing so in as clear and credible a way as possible

A fairly typical example can be found in the mid-1980s turnaround of the manufacturing and engineering part of Kodak's copier business.[5] Before the turnaround, most people knew there were problems; in 1984, it had to write off $40 million in inventory. But there was no alignment around a direction for solving those problems.

Kodak entered the copy business in the early 1970s and introduced its first product in 1975. The firm concentrated on the high end of the business, with technically sophisticated machines that sold, on average, for about $60,000 per unit. Over the next decade this business grew to nearly $1 billion in revenues. But costs were high, profits were hard to find, and problems were nearly everywhere.

All this began to change in late 1984 when Kodak's chairman, Colby Chandler, reorganized the company by line of business, breaking down huge functional hierarchies in the process. Two long-service Kodak employees with engineering degrees from Clarkson were given key jobs in the new copy products group; Chuck Trowbridge was appointed general manager and Bob Crandall was asked to run design and manufacturing.

In his first two months, Trowbridge met with nearly every key person inside his group as well as people elsewhere at Kodak that could be important to the copier business. He then worked with Cran-

dall and his other direct reports to formulate and articulate some
form of direction for the new division. Crandall, in turn, worked with
his own managers to formulate a vision and set of strategies for the
engineering and manufacturing organization. They then began to
create and use mechanisms for communicating that direction and for
convincing people they were seriously committed to making it a reality.

The essence of the manufacturing and engineering vision was really quite simple. If we are to stay in the copier business, they said, we
must undertake a journey toward becoming a world-class manufacturing operation, the type of operation that can produce a level of
quality, costs, and delivery accuracy that is magnitudes better than
our current performance. They later added, after that vision was
discussed again and again: To move toward world-class, we must
adopt a strategy of becoming less bureaucratic and more decentralized, so that we can give people both the responsibility and the ability
to improve quality, lower costs, and increase on-time deliveries.

Although simple, this message was difficult to convey because it
was such a radical departure from previous communications, not
only in the copy products organization, but throughout most of
Kodak. So Crandall set up dozens of vehicles to help emphasize and
re-emphasize the new direction. He started by meeting with all 100 of
his supervisors once every three months to talk about what improvements had been achieved and what projects were being launched to
create still better results. He set up quarterly "State of the Department" meetings where his managers met with everybody in their
own departments, such as stock control, to talk about similar things.
He held weekly meetings with his own twelve direct reports. He established something called "copy product forums," in which a different employee from each of his departments would meet together
with him as a group once a month just to talk.

Also, once a month, Crandall and all his direct reports would meet
with 80 to 100 people from some area of his organization, have coffee
and doughnuts, and talk about anything people wanted. More recently, he has created a format called "business meetings" where his
managers meet with 12 to 20 people to talk about some specific topic,
like inventory or master scheduling. The goal is to get all of his 1,500
employees in at least one of these focused "business meetings" each
year.

Written communication was also enlisted in this cause. A four- to
eight-page Copy Products Journal was sent to employees once a

month. People were encouraged to use the corporate-wide program called "Dialog Letters" which allowed employees to ask Crandall and other managers anything they wanted, anonymously, and be guaranteed a reply. But the most visible, and powerful, form of written communication were the charts. In a main hallway near the cafeteria, huge charts very clearly reported the quality, cost, and delivery results for each product against continuously difficult targets. A hundred smaller versions of these charts were scattered throughout the manufacturing area, reporting quality and costs for specific work groups.

Aside from his bosses, the single biggest unit outside of Crandall's organization that needed to be aligned to the new direction was the Kodak Apparatus Division, their biggest supplier by far, making about one-third of the parts they used. To get and keep the top management of that group on board, Crandall and his managers met with them over lunch every Thursday.

But perhaps most importantly, Crandall and his managers, with Trowbridge's support and help, talked constantly about where they were going, what progress they had been making, and what they were trying to do next. They talked with their people and with customers. They talked in meetings and in the hallways. They tried never to miss an opportunity to get their message across.

Some improved results were achieved within six months, more still after a year. These successes made their message more credible and helped get more people on board. When combined with another whole set of actions by Crandall and others to encourage, recognize, and reward people who were energetically pursuing the new direction, the performance improvements grew bigger and bigger.

Between 1984 and 1988, quality on one of their main product lines increased nearly one hundred-fold; defects per unit, before they were corrected at considerable expense, went from 30 to 0.3. Over a three-year period, costs on another product line went down nearly 24 percent. Deliveries on schedule went from 82 percent in 1985 to 95 percent in 1987. Inventory levels dropped by over 50 percent between 1984 and 1988 even though the volume of products was increasing. And productivity, measured in units per manufacturing employee, more than doubled from 1985 to 1988.

The sheer volume of communication, the repetition of a single message, and the focus on every relevant individual and group—all of this was only one aspect of the overall leadership process that produced these results. But it was an important part of the process and one that is often overlooked.

Crandall's huge charts, the ones in a busy hallway where everyone passes, are a good example of a communications vehicle almost always found in successful leadership stories. The concept is to find and use very simple images or words that communicate powerfully without clogging already overused communication channels or requiring a lot of scarce managerial time.

At NCR, Adamson also used charts on the production floor. His branch of the future, built right into the factory, communicated even more powerfully some messages that were central to the evolving Dundee vision and strategy. On the walls of the factory, Adamson hung posters that emphasized, usually in pictures, other directional themes. He also had a knack for selecting simple phrases that made some complex idea easy to remember: lowest total costs of ownership, fast-track development, the company-visit program.

At American Express, Lou Gerstner insisted that ways be found to reduce complicated strategies down to a minimum number of core principles. And like Adamson, he looked for simple but memorable ways to talk about those principles.

At SAS, Jan Carlzon was able to do the same thing with the phrase "best airline for the frequent business traveler." Not only are these seven words easy to remember, they actually helped people retain more detailed explanations of the new SAS strategy. So did another simple phrase he communicated often: "We used to fly planes; now we fly people."

Still another way Carlzon and his team communicated that strategy was with a booklet entitled "Let's Get In There and Fight" which they distributed to all 20,000 SAS employees. Unlike publications done with a purely managerial mind-set, this booklet did not contain page after page of printed words in small, single-space black type. It actually had relatively few words per page, all in large, readable type. Much of the message was delivered in pictures, cartoon-like drawings actually, which showed an airplane smiling, frowning, and covering its eyes with its wings. When Carlzon and his team first announced their intention to send out such a booklet, they ran into a torrent of dissent from managers who said it was too simplistic for their highly educated employees. They sent it anyway. And it worked.

Mary Kay Ash, about whom more will be said in the next chapter, is a master of symbolic communication. As the founder of one of the world's most successful skin care companies, she has given her firm a strong sense of direction for years now. Parts of that vision and strategy are continually communicated in many different ways, but some of the most powerful involve simple symbols.

Visitors to the Dallas headquarters of Mary Kay Cosmetics often find larger-than-life photographs of the firm's national sales directors. Those pictures, placed where they are, say more about the firm's competitive strategy than some corporations are able to say in thirty–page, usually unread, reports. The firm calls its independent sales agents "beauty consultants," two words that say a great deal about Mary Kay's whole approach to selling. One award that the corporation gives to successful beauty consultants is a 14-carat gold brooch in the shape of a bumblebee. The bumblebee, all new recruits are reminded, has a body too big for its wings and thus should not be able to fly. But it does. And that, they are told, is what this company is all about.

When John Harvey-Jones first became chairman of ICI, he decided to make the top management meeting place a visible symbol of the new style he felt was needed throughout the firm. Prior to Harvey-Jones, ICI's senior executives met regularly in their imposing, formal, magnificent board room. He immediately switched all meetings to the room that had been his office, a room in which he placed functional items like comfortable chairs and flip charts, and from which he removed all obvious symbols of formality and hierarchy.

The top management at Hewlett-Packard used architecture and design in an even stronger way when they built their corporate headquarters in Palo Alto in 1981 to 1982. To emphasize H-P's strategy of using expertise and good information, not titles, to determine key decisions, they built no conventional offices at all. Literally everyone in that building, even the CEO, was given a relatively modest open office, the kind with no floor-to-ceiling walls.

Perhaps the most obvious modern genius, when it comes to this type of communication, is a man who now lives a few hundred miles south of Hewlett-Packard headquarters. His name is Ronald Reagan, and even people who think he was a terrible President concede that he was most effective in conveying his vision for America. The key to that communication was the extremely effective use of short phrases, symbols, simple metaphors, and pictures. With these tools, he was able to say in ten minutes in his televised addresses and speeches what most of us convey, much less effectively, in an hour or more.

That capability made him, to friends and foes alike, "the great communicator."

Whether delivered with many words or a few carefully chosen symbols, messages are not necessarily accepted just because they are understood. A major challenge in leadership efforts is credibility—getting people to believe the message.

Many things contribute to credibility. The track record of the person delivering the message is extremely important in terms of both its strength and seeming relevance to the situation at hand. So is the content of the message itself, in terms of how sensible it seems; leaders often point to threats or potential threats to make the risks or sacrifices inherent in their vision seem rational. The reputation and relationships of the sending group are important, in terms of integrity and trustworthiness. So is consistency between the words and deeds of the communicator.

Few things can undermine the credibility of communication faster than a problem with consistency. People usually assume that actions do speak louder than words. As a result, one regularly finds in an effective leadership process a remarkable degree of congruence between the actions of key players and the message they communicate. Dick Nicolosi, the Procter & Gamble executive described later in Chapter 7, calls this "walking the talk."

At American Express, Lou Gerstner had a habit at management committee meetings of asking how specific proposals and actions fit or did not fit the TRS vision and strategies. When people came to talk to him in his office, he is said to have grown impatient unless they included something in the conversation that connected to the direction he was taking the firm. In a more general sense, he created a number of activities, in which he actively participated, that exemplified the vision and strategies. One of the most powerful of these is the Great Performers Program.

Started in 1980, Great Performers is an employee-recognition program that works like this. Anyone at TRS who sees an example of truly exceptional customer service, a central tenet in the organization's vision, can nominate the people who performed it to one of the Great Performers selection committees. Made up of a total of sixty people and divided into regional groups in 1987, these committees then research each nomination and select those that fit some standard of excellence. That year, 129 nominations were so selected. Complete details on each of these winners is then given to a Worldwide Governing Committee, chaired in 1987 by Aldo Papone and made up of eight top officers at TRS. They then select Grand Award Winners; there were twenty-six of these in 1987. Regular winners receive a plaque, some money, a gold "GP" logo pin, and a letter of commendation from the president of their regional selection committee, all of which is usually presented by senior management of the location where the employee works. Grand Award Winners receive the plaque, the pin, $4,000 in American Express traveler's checks, and an all-expenses paid trip to New York.

In 1987, Lyndon Deane and Carrie Lee Lewis were two of the Grand Award Winners. Lyndon, 23–years–old, worked in the Telephone Service Center in Toronto, and Carrie, twenty-seven, worked in the TRS travel office in Saskatchewan, Canada. They won for helping an American Express customer whose son was seriously injured in an accident in Brazil. When Carrie heard of the problem the client was having, she arranged for funds to be transferred from Canada to Brazil for the emergency. When the client decided to bring the boy home for treatment, she made all the flight arrangements. Air Canada insisted that a paramedic accompany the boy on the flight, but on the night before his flight the paramedic discovered that he would need a visa. Lyndon somehow arranged for the visa to be issued on a Saturday, picked it up, and then personally transported the paramedic to the airport in his car.

Mildred Asencio and five of her colleagues from the Puerto Rico Service Center were also winners. They volunteered to set up an American Express desk on New Year's Eve to help the victims of the tragic Dupont Plaza Hotel fire. Sherri Kline of Phoenix won for helping the police arrest people who were exploiting an elderly and mentally handicapped customer. Amin Hitti of Beirut, Lebanon, won for a long list of services performed despite the constant threat of personal violence.

The New York trip for Carrie, Lyndon, Amin, and the other winners was quite an event. They stayed at a luxury hotel, saw Broadway shows, ate in some of the best restaurants, and were presented their other awards at a luncheon hosted by TRS senior management on one of the top floors of the American Express tower in the World Financial Center.

The luncheon for 1987 Grand Award Winners was held on February 23, 1988 from 12:00 to 2:15 P.M. It began with a cocktail reception, followed by an elegant lunch and then the awards ceremony. Each of the top eight TRS executives took part in the ceremony by describing the "great performance" of two or three individuals or groups and then by giving them their awards. There was much applause and a lot of misty eyes. Gerstner ended the ceremony with a short speech about how some of his managers had just given him a party to celebrate his tenth year with TRS, and at that party had presented him with a plaque like the one that everyone in the room had just received. This was an award, he clearly showed, of which he was very proud.

No doubt the whole event was a source of inspiration for the twenty-six winners. But after news of the ceremony was broadcast throughout TRS in house newsletters, speeches, and informal gossip, the contest became a powerful force for alignment for thousands of employees. The message—about how serious senior management was when it said it wanted to become better at customer service than *any* competitor—was powerful and very clear.

Powerful messages are communicated to employees by executive behavior all the time in most organizations. Unfortunately, unlike this TRS situation, those messages often do not help generate understanding and support for some future direction. The communication that is frequently received is either a) there is no vision or strategy here, or b) we are not really committed to the vision and strategies we have been asking you to embrace. The impact in both cases is deadly.

One of the reasons organizations have difficulty adjusting to market or technological change is that so many people in those firms feel relatively powerless. They have learned from experience, that even if they correctly perceive important external changes and then initiate appropriate actions, they are vulnerable to someone higher in the hierarchy that does not like what they have done. Reprimands can take a hundred different forms: that is against policy; we can't afford to do that; shut up and do as you're told.

Alignment helps overcome this problem by empowering people in at least two different ways.[6] First, when a clear sense of direction has been communicated throughout an organization, it allows even lower-level employees to initiate actions without that same degree of vulnerability; as long as their behavior is consistent with the vision, superiors will have more difficulty reprimanding them. Second, because everyone is aiming at the same target, the probability is less that a single person's initiative will be stalled because it comes into conflict with someone else's.

In a relatively stable environment, people empowered in this way

Exhibit 4.2 *Aligning People*

Alignment	A condition in which a relevant group of people share a common understanding of a vision and set of strategies, accept the validity of that direction, and are willing to work toward making it a reality
Creating alignment	Communicating the direction as often as possible (repetition is important) to all those people (subordinates, subordinates of subordinates, bosses, suppliers, etc.) whose help or cooperation is needed; doing so, whenever possible, with simple images or symbols or metaphors that communicate powerfully without clogging already overused communications channels and without requiring a lot of scarce managerial time; making the message credible by using communicators with good track records and working relationships, by stating the message in as sensible a way as possible, by making sure the words and deeds of the communicators are consistent, and generally by demonstrating an unswerving dedication to the vision and strategies (so-called "leadership by example")
Potential impact	An aligned group of people has the potential of making progress toward some vision.

can contribute a modest amount. In a rapidly changing environment, those same individuals can be invaluable. That is one more reason why alignment (see summary in Exhibit 4.2) is so important today.

5

Motivating and Inspiring

When trying to produce a change of any significance, people aligned to even the most sensible of directions almost always encounter serious barriers, some of which can be extremely hard to foresee in advance. These roadblocks can be economic; a million dollars is suddenly needed but nowhere to be found. Often they are bureaucratic or political; a department refuses to answer an urgent request in less than its usual two-month response time.

Getting over, around, or through barriers to change can demand extraordinary energy and effort. Obtaining a million dollars quickly might require people to work all night and to work with an intensity of imagination that is anything but normal. Getting a recalcitrant department to respond in a week instead of two months may well require an unusually inspired effort from somebody. Indeed, with anything less than highly motivated behavior, these kinds of barriers can stop an entire "change effort" or slow it to a crippling pace—even if appropriate people are aligned to a sensible direction.

Since change is the primary function of leadership, being able to generate highly energized behavior is as centrally important here as are direction setting and alignment. In a sense, direction setting identifies an appropriate path for movement, effective alignment gets people moving down that path, and a successful motivational effort assures that those people will have the energy to overcome obstacles in their way.

To understand this aspect of leadership, it is once again useful to look at management, where motivation is also a relevant topic. But the kind of motivation that applies to management is very different from the kind that applies to leadership.

The basic function of management is homeostatic; it is to keep a system alive by making sure that critical variables remain within tolerable ranges constantly.[1] Thus, the complex mechanism that manages the human body keeps the temperature close to 98 degrees Fahrenheit, and does so twenty-four hours a day, week after week. In a similar way, managerial processes in a well-run factory keep product quality consistently within an acceptable range. The same kind of processes in a well-run marketing department keep projects on or near budget, all the time.

An important aspect of any homeostatic process is control. After a target has been established and a system has been designed that can achieve that target, a control mechanism is created to monitor continuously system behavior versus plan and then to take action when a deviation is detected. In a well-managed factory, this means the planning process establishes sensible quality targets, the organizing process builds an organization that can achieve those targets, and a control process makes sure that quality lapses are spotted immediately, not in thirty or sixty days, and corrected. In a well-managed marketing department, a project that goes over budget will get the same treatment.

One way that management achieves control is by "motivating" people to comply with the standards or the plan. This is often done with economic incentives—that is, a certain amount of compensation is made contingent on a person's ability to minimize deviations from plan, or at least unfavorable deviations. Sometimes management tries to achieve this more informally, through group norms and pressures. But the end or goal is the same: control.

For some of the same reasons that control is so central to management, highly motivated or inspired behavior is almost irrelevant. Because they are called upon to produce expected results constantly, managerial processes must be as close as possible to fail-safe and risk-free. That, in turn, means they cannot be dependent on the unusual or hard to obtain. Thus, a good budgeting process does not require Einstein to run it. A well-organized personnel department does not need all-night vigils once a week to get the routine job done. In a sense, the whole purpose of systems and structures is to help normal people who behave in normal ways to complete routine jobs successfully, day after day. It's not exciting or glamorous. ment.

Leadership is different. Achieving grand visions cles always requires an occasional burst of energy tain motivational and inspirational processes processes accomplish their energizing effect, not in the right direction, as a control mechanism oft isfying very basic human needs: for achievement, belonging, recognition, self-esteem, a sense of control over one's life, and living up to one's ideals. These processes touch us deeply and powerfully, and elicit a most powerful response.

The motivational aspect of leadership can manifest itself in many different ways. But more often than not, it comes in a package that includes 1) the articulation of a vision in a manner that stresses the values of the audience being addressed (and thus makes the work important to these individuals), 2) the involvement of those people in deciding how to achieve that vision or the part of the vision that is most relevant to them (giving people a sense of control), 3) the enthusiastic support of their efforts at achieving that vision, supplemented by coaching, feedback, and role modeling (which helps them grow professionally and enhances their self-esteem), and 4) the public recognition and rewarding of all their successes (providing them with recognition, a sense of belonging to an organization that cares about them, and a feeling of accomplishment). In a sense, when this is done, the work itself seems intrinsically motivating.[2]

These four elements can be all found in the NCR story. They are also present, to some degree, in a full account of the TRS, SAS, and Kodak cases. They generated forces that helped Adamson, Gerstner, Carlzon, and Crandall overcome major barriers that stood between them and their visions. They were centrally important to the production of important results, although in a manner that is completely different from the control aspect of management.

A control process seeks to minimize deviations from plan so as to produce consistent results. The kind of motivational process relevant to leadership tries to maximize energy output so as to overcome barriers to change. The former is cautious and conservative, the latter bold, perhaps even brash. Controls are purely driven by the head, whereas inspiration often comes from the heart. The one focuses on surface behavior and its effects, the other on the deepest reaches of the human soul. They can both be difficult, and more and more are needed everywhere in organizations, but they are definitely different (see Exhibit 5.1).

All this may seem painfully obvious, but it most certainly is not to certain kinds of people. Indeed, a person who has been socialized only into a managerial way of thinking and behaving will often approach motivation in a manner that cannot possibly support high energy levels. To motivate, he or she will try to increase people's efforts to accomplish precisely what is on his or her agenda by offering incentives, carrots and sticks, in a highly controlling manner. He will smile or praise every time people do something called for in his plan. He will frown or punish if they do not. He will orchestrate meetings in which people are asked for their opinions, which are then twisted until they precisely fit his preexisting plan, all in an effort to "excite through involvement." He will offer extra monetary or other rewards, but always with a hundred conditions designed to channel behavior exactly where he wants it.

This approach to motivating can produce an energy surge in a naive audience for a short period of time, but that is all. Over the long term, it always fails. People see this behavior as highly manipulative, and come to resent it greatly. Ultimately, it demotivates.

Usually, this same type of person will not even try to inspire.[3] He or she will sense that inspiration is explosive, and thus hard to control. As such, he will question whether it should ever be used or if it is ever really needed. And he certainly will not understand how it is done.

Exhibit 5.1 *Execution: Management vs. Leadership*

	Management: Controlling & Problem Solving	Leadership: Motivating & Inspiring
Function	To minimize deviations from plan, and thus help produce predictable results on important dimensions	To energize people to overcome major obstacles toward achieving a vision, and thus to help produce the change needed to cope with a changing environment
A brief description of the activity	Monitoring results versus plan in some detail, both formally and informally, by means of reports, meetings, and other control mechanisms, identifying deviations from plan, which are usually called "problems," and then planning and organizing to solve those problems	Satisfying very basic but often unfulfilled human needs—for achievement, belonging, recognition, self-esteem, a sense of control over one's life, living up to one's ideals—and thereby creating an unusually high energy level in people

All this means, among other things, is that such a person will find a company like Mary Kay Cosmetics very strange.

Mary Kay Cosmetics was founded in 1963 by Mary Kay Ash.[4] By 1989, it had grown to be one of the most successful firms in its industry anywhere in the world. At the core of its success is a highly motivated distribution system, made up mainly of women, who both sell its products and recruit and train other sales people. Many other firms think they have highly motivated sales forces. But just one trip to Dallas, when Mary Kay is having its yearly convention, is usually enough to show that, by comparison at least, few really do.

During the summer of 1988, nearly 32,000 Mary Kay beauty consultants and sales directors descended on Dallas, all at their own expense.[5] They came 8,000 at a time, the capacity limit for the event, to learn from each other, to have fun, to receive awards, and generally to get inspired. Sales conventions have a tendency to be very visible and a little loud, and this one is no exception. It's easy to spot the Mary Kay people, whether in a hotel or in a downtown store. They seem to be singing everywhere, even on airplanes going to or coming from Dallas. But normal sales gatherings are also often very annoying to the outside observer. People drink too much. Things eventually become a little crude. Not so at Mary Kay.

At a Mary Kay sales convention people are truly joyful. The energy and enthusiasm are incredibly upbeat, positive, powerful, and infectious. It is hard not to smile when you see these people, or to feel some excitement. They look like they could conquer the world, and some do; despite all the difficult obstacles encountered in direct selling and in building a direct selling organization, Mary Kay has more women associated with it who earn over $50,000 a year than any other corporation on earth.[6]

The structure of the three-day affair is relatively simple. Most of the time is scheduled around seminar classes. Attendees learn about the firm and its products, as well as about selling, recruiting new talent, training new recruits, and motivating people. There are plenty of social events too, and awards seem to be handed out all the time. But the main non-seminar session is Awards Night, when the biggest prizes are given to consultants with the biggest sales. Hundreds of prizes are given. Some are very expensive, some not, but all are accompanied with thunderous applause, and interspersed with touchingly inspirational speeches from very ordinary people who have become very successful. This is the kind of evening that increases the heartbeat and moistens the eye of all but the most cynical among us.

The stylistic details of Awards Night are unique to Mary Kay, but the concept of a grand yearly awards ceremony is not. What sets this firm apart from so many others is its approach to people between conventions. At Mary Kay Cosmetics, management works not 3 but 365 days a year to try to arouse that "90 percent" which they believe remains "untapped" in most people. And they do so in dozens of ways that look remarkably unsophisticated in our high-tech age.

They send birthday cards to everyone. When someone comes to them with an idea or a problem, they really try to listen. When they promise to do something, they usually do it, and in a timely fashion. If an individual is having a performance problem, they try to help the person improve, or if that isn't sensible, to get him or her a more appropriate job either inside the company or somewhere else.

They are enthusiastic about what they do. One gets a sense that they believe in the company and its vision, are proud to be associated with both, and genuinely like each other. Continually, they sponsor events that bring people together. And they actually do sing at these events.

The top people at Mary Kay work hard at being good role models and at providing forums in which more senior sales directors or beauty consultants can act as role models for others. Time and again they find ways to allow successful people to tell their stories to others. Some of these stories, about individuals who started with little money or hope, are really extraordinary. (The leadership process in the firm produces the ultimate in change—it alters people's lives.)

They do everything practical to help people succeed. Sales directors work with new recruits to get them started and to help them set realistic goals. They offer training and coaching. They structure the beauty consultant's job to give people as much control over their own destinies as possible.

Even between conventions, they give out prizes for excellent performance. At the annual meeting and elsewhere, awards are usually high quality items that their people really want and value: a luxury car, a trip on the Concorde to Europe, a beautiful piece of jewelry. They almost always give rewards in public ceremonies that include a great deal of sincere applause.

In many ways, it is all thoroughly old-fashioned. But it works because it appeals to something as old as our species: basic human nature. Mary Kay Ash and her management understand that people want to feel good about themselves but often do not because a variety of basic human needs are unsatisfied. They also know that when an individual or a company is able somehow to help people satisfy a number of these needs, normal human beings often turn into dynamos. It is the psychological equivalent of giving a starving man, who cannot even walk, well-balanced meals.

The way in which Mary Kay does all this often looks spontaneously haphazard. It is not. Underlying what they do is a very systematic approach: they constantly communicate the firm's vision in ways that might inspire people; they empower individuals to pursue that vision by giving real responsibility to them, by helping them to master that responsibility, and by trying not to do anything that would discourage them; then they recognize and reward every success. This simple formula provides people with self-confidence, a sense of achievement, self-esteem, a sense of belonging, some control over their lives, a feeling of working for a worthy cause, and from that, enormous energy to help them overcome the barriers they encounter constantly in their jobs.

The style with which the formula is enacted is, to a large degree, uniquely Mary Kay. But the substance goes far beyond this single situation. Wherever you find competent leadership, you find some of the Mary Kay phenomenon. It is usually more focused, because barriers to change are normally more concentrated in time and space. But it is there. When you find truly exceptional leadership, you usually will find lots of this phenomenon.

Wal-Mart is a good example. This extraordinary company has recently become the second most profitable retailer in the United States, despite the fact that it is less than thirty years old.[7] It has won that distinction by beating thousands of small retailers, as well as K-Mart, Zayre, Penney's, and dozens of other large retail chains. The story of its success has many aspects, but none is more important than the motivation of its people; the energy level of the firm's employees is awesome. Well managed and well led, Wal-Mart understands the Mary Kay phenomena in a way that is very rare among large U.S. corporations today. And the payoff, to customers, employees, and stockholders, has been fantastic.

Another good example of the use of this basic motivational scheme, and one far more typical than Mary Kay or Wal-Mart, is that of Kentucky Fried Chicken.[8] There it has helped CEO Dick Mayer turn a shrinking business doing $1.5 billion in revenues in 1978, and filled with problems, into a growing and profitable enterprise that had revenues of nearly $5 billion in 1988.

Kentucky Fried Chicken's roots date back to 1939 when Colonel Harland Sanders began selling fried chicken prepared with his recipe of eleven herbs and spices at the restaurant he owned in Corbin, Kentucky. The firm was incorporated in 1955 to franchise the Colonel's recipe, and by the time he sold the business in 1964 to a group of investors, there were 600 restaurants. In 1971, ownership was acquired by Heublein. As a division of a firm whose main product was vodka, the restaurant chain began to experience an increasing number of problems. To turn things around, Heublein assigned Mike Miles and Dick Mayer,[9] both of whom had had considerable experience in the packaged food business, to Kentucky Fried Chicken. Over the next decade, the new management team stopped the downward trend, established the foundations of a well-managed corporation, and then started innovating to produce more profitable growth.

An episode in the firm's history that began in 1985 is illustrative of how Kentucky Fried Chicken has managed to overcome obstacles that stop or slow progress at so many firms.* By that time, Mayer was well aware that achieving his vision of a growing and increasingly profitable enterprise would require the building of a strong lunch business for his restaurants and the attraction of more young customers. A number of events that year led him to begin studying what other restaurant chains did at lunch. Encouraged by what he saw, he asked market research specialist Harry Sunenshine to conduct a more formal investigation. Then, in January 1986, Mayer and Sunenshine met to share their analyses.

Of all the data they had collected, two facts struck them as particularly interesting. At McDonald's, the most successful restaurant chain in the world, especially with young people, 53 percent of its hamburger revenue came from one product: not the relatively expensive Big Mac or Quarter Pounder, but the least expensive, single hamburger. At White Castle, a successful regional chain with 225 stores, revenues per store were as good as McDonald's despite the fact that it sold only one sandwich, a twenty-nine cent hamburger. Additional data from the experiences of other chains reinforced this pattern

---

*However, it is not illustrative of its business successes over the past decade; as of this writing, and for a variety of reasons, the Chicken Littles product has failed to achieve even half the sales volume that was originally projected.

about the appeal of a good but low-cost sandwich, especially to younger customers. All this led Mayer and Sunenshine to conclude that an inexpensive chicken sandwich should probably be the initial vehicle for building a luncheon business—other sandwiches at various prices would come next. They also decided that the best way to pursue this course in a firm without a good track record for new product introductions, and in an industry that was fast to copy, was quietly and quickly.

Within the next week, Mayer met individually with Ed Dudley, vice-president of purchasing and manufacturing, Phil Bouckaert, vice-president of technology, Don Doyle, president of KFC-USA, and Roger Kramer, vice-president of strategic planning. He also contacted Shelby Massey, vice-chairman at Tyson, the giant poultry and meat company. In each of these conversations, Mayer talked at length about the concept: why the time was right to start building a lunch business, which, if successful, could significantly increase sales and profitability; what an analysis of restaurant sandwich and lunch business seems to indicate; why they should probably create a totally new sandwich product, something inexpensive, with a high value/price ratio, that would draw people to their restaurants for lunch. He also talked about his belief that this project could be an important and exciting episode in Kentucky Fried Chicken's history, and about how it could represent the beginning of a more innovative period. He ended each meeting by stressing how critically important each of them would be to the success of the project: Dudley by working with suppliers to develop the chicken patty, the bun, and the new equipment that would be needed in the restaurants; Bouckaert for operations engineering at the store level and for the development of the overall product; Sunenshine for the additional competitive research needed to develop a marketing position and strategy; Massey for bringing all of Tyson's expertise in poultry to bear on the project. He also stressed the need for secrecy; for now, the project would be known as "Project X" and not even their secretaries should be informed.

During the next month, each of these executives began developing their pieces of Project X, urged on by an always enthusiastic Dick Mayer. A few more people were brought into this secret society, including Bill Davis, the CEO of Hobart, a kitchen equipment manufacturing firm; John Bellert, the chief engineer for KFC; and Pat Hadden, one of Bellert's subordinates. Mayer also briefed the parent company's board of directors. In each of these cases, Mayer's capacity to talk logically about the facts and to talk enthusiastically about the possibilities, when combined with the credibility he had developed at KFC, was very powerful. Most people quickly became "believers."

Mayer stayed in close contact with each of the team members. He encouraged them to come to him at any time if they needed additional help or resources. With his encouragement and support, product and equipment development proceeded on an extremely fast track during March of 1986, with Hobart, Tyson, and the KFC people overcoming a number of technical problems. At this time, Mayer personally worked with John McGarry, chairman of Young & Rubicam-New York, on a name for the product and on advertising copy. As momentum began to develop, so did a sense of excitement among those involved. At the end of the month, Mayer tantalized the National Convention of KFC Franchises by announcing that they were working on something important that had the potential for considerable growth beyond the current business, but stopped short of giving any details.

By April 8, the first advertising copy using the name "Chicken Littles" was completed and reviewed with Ed Dudley. Unfortunately, a quick search by Steve Early, general counsel for KFC, determined that the name was trademarked and owned by two other companies. Mayer and his people decided the name was too good to abandon, so they gave Dudley a budget and told him that it was essential that he secure rights to that name, no matter what. During this time, the patty production process and bun requirements were further defined, a griddle was developed by Hobart, and market research was conducted in Columbus, Ohio, and Charlotte, North Carolina, on a grilled sandwich.

The market research results arrived on May 15, but they were not good. Mayer allowed no time for people to get discouraged; he immediately challenged Sunenshine and Bouckaert to study the research data to find what it says about a better product. They did, and a number of alternatives were developed and tested. One fried sandwich tested especially well. Mayer then enlisted the help of food technologist Dr. G. V. Rao in further developing that alternative.

In June, Mayer made a formal presentation on Project X to the parent company's board. In July, he met with two small elected groups representing franchises, gave them a complete briefing, and asked for their ideas and comments. During August, a few more people were brought into the project team, each to handle specific, essential tasks.

In September, the team found a piece of equipment, sold by Vulcan-Hart, that could make the fried version of Chicken Littles. They also switched bun suppliers after the initial selection ran into problems. In October, they prepared for and ran a test of the product and equipment in one store. In November, thirty franchise owners were brought to Louisville for a day-long briefing on Project X. In December, they made preparations to introduce Chicken Littles at the twenty-two stores in the Louisville area. That introduction occurred, on schedule, the first week of January 1987. And, to the delight of everyone involved, most customers loved the product.

Mayer invited as many franchise owners to Louisville as he could, so they could see for themselves how the public was reacting to the sandwich. Nearly fifty came, including some of the most influential ones. He and other KFC officers personally took them to the Louisville stores at lunchtime to see the product being sold, the customers, and the excitement. Everyone walked away from these encounters feeling good, especially the people who had been working so hard to make Chicken Littles a reality.

In February, more and more time was spent working with suppliers on huge logistical tasks. Tyson was building additional capacity to make the chicken patty. Flowers Bakery was upgrading and enhancing its bun operations in Fresno California, Texarkana, Morristown Tennessee, Atlanta, and Orlando. Amana was building the microwave ovens that would be needed in the restaurants, Delfield, the sandwich tables, and Vulcan-Hart, the fryers.

In March, Mayer, Doyle, Sunenshine, Bouckaert, and Dudley made a presentation to Wayne Calloway, the chairman of their new parent corporation (KFC was sold to PepsiCo while all of this was occurring), and asked for a $6 million commitment to continue the project. Calloway reacted enthusiastically to what he heard, praised them for their efforts, and gave them the money.

In April, the franchises held their annual convention in Louisville. It was quite an affair. Mayer made a presentation of the Chicken Littles concept. He told them about the test results. He showed them advertising developed for the product. And he introduced the key people who had been working on Project X, including representatives from all the major suppliers. It was great theater, and the franchise owners loved it. After all the applause was over, Mayer asked for an additional allocation from them to support national advertising for the new sandwich. As was the custom in these cases, they voted. Ninety percent said yes.

During May, KFC people went on the road to train franchises in the use of the new equipment and the new product. They worked long hours, traveling all over the country to the firm's 4,000 restaurants. When they completed their task in August, Don Doyle had a big party for all of them in Louisville. With Mayer and others also in attendance, members of the road team told their favorite stories or tales about what had happened to them over the last few months. Some of the stories were hilarious. It was quite a celebration.

By August 8, some 97 percent of the KFC outlets were serving Chicken Littles. In an industry that takes two to three years to introduce a totally new product,* KFC accomplished this in eighteen months. An energized group of people overcame hundreds of technical, economic, logistical, legal, and political obstacles and they did so with remarkable speed.

Adamson would have been proud of them. They took his fast track development and made it work in the multi-unit restaurant business.

Motivating people for a short period of time is not very difficult. A crisis will often do just that, or a carefully planned special event. Motivating people over a longer period of time, however, is far more difficult. It is also far more important in today's business environment.

Motivation over time requires, first, that visions and strategies be communicated on a continuous basis, not just once or occasionally. (Mayer probably gave some version of his we-see-an-opportunity-for-a-new-lunch business speech well over 100 times.) That communication must go beyond just informing; it must excite people by connecting to their values. (From Mayer's first conversations with Bouckaert and Doyle to his presentation a year later at the franchisees convention, people usually walked away not only understanding the concept but feeling enthusiastic about it.) People's involvement in deciding how to implement the vision must be real, not manipulative. (Mayer consistently gave his people considerable leeway, trusting that they would deliver.) The right kind of support must be forthcoming so that individuals can succeed in making progress toward that vision. (In Mayer's case, he encouraged people to come to him at any time if they needed help, he always provided financial and human resources when they were needed, he cheered people onward with

---

*This is one that requires new suppliers and equipment.

Exhibit 5.2 *Motivating and Inspiring*

Motivated/ inspired people	A group of people who exhibit a level of energy, intensity, and determination far above what is considered normal. In a successful leadership effort this level of motivation tends to be sustained for relatively long periods of time.
Creating motivation and inspiration	Satisfying very basic human needs for achievement, belonging, recognition, self-esteem, a sense of control over one's life, living up to one's ideals, etc.; by 1) articulating again and again a vision in a way that stresses the key values of the people being communicated to, 2) involving those people in deciding how to achieve that vision or some portion of the vision, 3) supporting their efforts with coaching, feedback, role modeling, and a lot of of enthusiasm, and 4) sincerely recognizing in public and rewarding all of their successes.
Potential impact	A highly motivated group that is aligned to some direction can overcome major economic, bureaucratic, and political obstacles that stand in its way.

tremendous enthusiasm, and he generally modeled the kind of leadership he wanted from them.) And the rewards and recognition must be sincere. (At KFC they were: the daily pats on the back, praising people's accomplishments at the franchisees convention, throwing a party for the "road team," to mention but a few.)

Again, corporations that are well led understand all this (see Exhibit 5.2). But there are far too few of these firms today.

III

The Structure of Leadership

6

Multiple Roles

When considering the topic of leadership, we typically think of one leader. The logical connection is straightforward; it is one individual, most people believe, that creates leadership. In this causal model, the structure of leadership, that is, the roles involved and their interrelationships, is elegantly simple. There are only two roles: leader and follower. They are related in an almost hierarchical way through the leadership process; a leader establishes a direction, aligns followers to that direction, and then inspires them to action.

This way of conceptualizing the structure of leadership is popular because it is simple, yet powerful, in seeming to explain so many situations. The Adamson story from Chapter 2, for example, obviously appears to fit this model. So do the TRS and SAS cases, the Chrysler turnaround under Lee Iacocca, as well as thousands of other lesser known stories. But appearances can be deceiving. Probing beneath the surface, one finds that this simple model does not do an adequate job of explaining leadership situations in large settings. In such cases, there are often more than two roles involved, sometimes many more.[1] And the relationship between the various leader and follower roles is far more complicated.

Probing still deeper, one finds that the basic model does not explain everything even in relatively small situations. It does not, for example, fit all of the Adamson story. If it did, when he was away from Dundee from January 1986 to June 1987, the leadership he created would have disappeared. But it did not. It may have dampened in its intensity, or changed its shape somewhat, but it clearly did not disappear.

   To understand leadership in complex organizations, it is essential to appreciate the structurally complex ways it can manifest itself. Such an understanding has powerful action implications for those who wish to increase the amount of leadership in corporations.

ARCO's success in the 1980s with its so-called "restructuring program" is a good example of a leadership story that does not fit the one-leader-plus-followers model.[2]

   ARCO, the Los Angeles-based energy company, was built by legendary oil entrepreneur Robert O. Anderson. The "restructuring program" refers to a number of actions taken between 1982 and 1986 which, in total, changed the economic and financial structure of the corporation fairly dramatically. Echoing the sentiments of many observers, *Business Week* has called the program "one of the boldest such moves in recent years [and] a huge success."[3]

   The most visible part of this restructuring came in a package announced on April 29, 1985. On that day, ARCO management informed the world that they were selling almost all of Anaconda Copper, as well as all of their oil refining and marketing assets east of the Mississippi, moves that would require a $1.5 billion write-off, but would rid them of chronically under-performing businesses. They also pledged to undertake a major cost-cutting campaign in their remaining businesses and to buy back $4 billion worth of their own stock.

   There were at least five other less visible aspects of the overall program. One came in August 1984, when the firm took a $750 million write-off, mostly associated with divesting parts of the copper business, and bought back $1 billion worth of stock. Another initiative in 1984 involved merging and reorganizing the Houston refinery and chemical plant into a relatively independent unit called the Lyondell Petrochemical Company. A third action came in late 1985, when management sold a number of marginal U.S. oil-producing properties.

   Occurring over a span of time between 1982 and 1986 and focusing on the refinery and selling of gas in the western United States, the final actions connected with the restructuring were more incremental in nature. These included eliminating the gasoline credit card in April 1982, more aggressively converting service stations to self-service with AM/PM mini-grocery stores, and a thousand small changes to boost output at the Los Angeles and Washington refineries without major capital investments—actions that together allowed

ARCO to lower its prices and increase its market share in the West from fourth place in 1981 to first place in 1988.[4]

The net result of all of this was a much changed company. After restructuring, ARCO was a smaller, more focused, and more efficient firm that was capable of producing higher returns on assets and equity, even in a world with oil prices much lower than they were in the early 1980s. In 1981, ARCO's ROE was 10 points below Occidental Petroleum's and nearly even with that of Exxon, Chevron, and AMOCO. By late 1987, after oil prices had plummeted to nearly $10 a barrel from a high of $32, ARCO's ROE had risen to 23 percent, while that of all the others had gone down, leaving the firm a full 7 ROE points ahead of second-place Exxon.[5] A variety of other leadership initiatives combined with this restructuring to push ROE results even higher in 1988,[6] and higher still the first half of 1989.

Without effective leadership, as everyone close to this story agrees, these results would not exist. But a careful examination of the facts reveals that leadership was not centered around a single individual. A number of different people played very important roles. In the restructuring story, this starts with Ron Arnault.

Arnault joined ARCO in 1969 after receiving an MBA from Wharton. From 1977 to 1980, he served as the corporate vice-president for planning. From 1980 to 1984 he was president of ARCO Ventures/Solar, and in 1984 he became the firm's chief financial officer. More than any other single individual, Arnault was responsible for setting the course for restructuring. Working with a team of ARCO executives in finance, planning, and legal, along with the investment banking firm of Salomon Brothers, Arnault put together facts supporting the necessity of restructuring: how the firm was overcapitalized, how Anaconda and certain other assets were underperforming, how all this made ARCO vulnerable to a raider. He and his team also identified various ways that the restructuring could be approached, analyzed the possible economic consequences of different approaches, and then worked at communicating these ideas to key ARCO executives. Their success in convincing Bill Kieschnick, the president of ARCO from 1981 to 1985, was a particularly important part of the story.

Lod Cook, executive vice-president in 1983, president in 1985, and chairman in 1986, did not need much convincing. From nearly the beginning, the restructuring ideas made sense to him, and he helped shape some of them as they evolved from 1984 to 1986. But in the sense that Arnault took the lead in setting the direction for restructuring, Cook took the lead in getting people lined up behind those ideas and in motivating them to make it all happen.

A soft-spoken southerner, Cook joined ARCO in 1956 shortly after graduating from Louisiana State University with a degree in petroleum engineering. He worked for nearly fourteen years in personnel/labor relations before taking on a number of marketing and general management assignments. During the early part of the restructuring story, he played a key role in getting ARCO executives, including Chairman Robert Anderson, behind the evolving effort and keeping them behind it. In the latter stages of the story, he became the firm's chief spokesman for explaining restructuring decisions to ARCO employees and for instilling enthusiasm about making the new ARCO function.

Convincing employees to embrace restructurings of this kind is never easy. In the fall of 1985, Cook began what became an ongoing series of meetings with groups of people throughout the corporation. He explained his own version of the restructuring, acknowledged the trauma that this created for many employees, but urged them to see the future benefits. He almost always allowed a lengthy period for questions, and encouraged people to speak up, even if that meant hostile inquiries. His candid, low-key, non-intimidating, but well-informed approach to these sessions was very effective.

Robert O. Anderson, the entrepreneur that built ARCO and the chairman prior to Cook, played a relatively minor role in all this, at least compared to Arnault's and Cook's. But it was a centrally important role, and undoubtedly not an easy one for him. Restructuring meant changing the direction of the firm in some fundamental ways, a direction that Anderson had personally set and maintained for two decades. Unlike the vast majority of strong entrepreneurial leaders who build firms but then forever refuse to see the need for a change in direction, Anderson helped Arnault and others shape the restructuring package, played a leading part in convincing the board to support these ideas, turned over the reins to Cook, and retired from ARCO.[7]

Credit for the fact that Anderson actually played a leadership role in the restructuring, as opposed to being a barrier to change, goes first to Anderson himself, an extraordinary individual. But others helped him line up behind these ideas and become comfortable with them, especially the thought of selling the Anaconda acquisition that

Anderson himself made. Cook was important in this sense, as was Kieschnick.

Bill Kieschnick was president under Anderson from 1981 to 1985. A chemical engineer by training, Kieschnick quickly embraced the restructuring concept and worked hard to keep the new direction-setting process alive and moving, and to get Anderson, along with the key ARCO people, behind it. At the beginning, in particular, Kieschnick was the engine that kept the process going; without him, it may well have stalled.

After Kieschnick, Cook, Arnault, and Anderson, there is a longer list of people who played even more specific, but nonetheless important, roles in this story. George Babikian and Jim Morrison provided strong leadership in the marketing side of the oil business. Important work by them was even done well before Arnault started talking about the restructuring theme. Employee relations personnel designed and implemented an innovative early retirement program that helped enormously in the process. Still others led efforts to increase productivity at the Washington and Los Angeles refineries, to make the new Lyondell Petrochemical Company a money maker, and to reduce overhead in various staff units.

Overall, it is hard to pinpoint how many people played some type of leadership role of consequence in this story. Three or four clearly had very big parts. At least another dozen contributed in other important ways. But none of these people played the single leader role that is inherent in the most common model we employ to conceptualize leadership. Instead, they were all more specialized, in a sense. Some were specialized in terms of some aspect of the leadership process itself, focusing mostly, for example, on direction setting or one element of the alignment process. Others were specialized in terms of some aspect of the story—such as providing broad restructuring leadership for the products (gas, oil) marketing organization or for the new petrochemical company in Houston.

The overall pattern of role specialization is complex and, to a large degree, very idiosyncratic to this specific story. But the degree and amount of specialization is not at all unusual. It happens, and happens often, out of necessity.

The role Jim Adamson handled so well in Dundee was an extremely difficult one. Yet in terms of scale, the situation at ARCO was 50 to 200 times larger.[8] Perhaps the business equivalent of Churchill or

Gandhi could have been a successful Adamson at ARCO. But it is far more logical, in a situation like this, to expect to find a group of very talented individuals supplying the overall leadership, all in somewhat differentiated roles. The magnitude of the task simply demands it.

It is not unlike the case with "management." Organizations today normally ask, not one, but many people to help with management, because that task is so large and complex. In the past ten to fifteen years, the leadership challenge in most industries has grown to be almost equally as large, if not larger, and the needed response, as the ARCO case shows, is very much the same. Indeed, in firms like ARCO, more and more people are being asked to play both leadership and management roles, though the demands of each are quite different (see Exhibit 6.1).

Even in relatively small organizations, multiple people play both

Exhibit 6.1 *Management and Leadership Roles*

	Management Roles	Leadership Roles
Purpose	To create management processes, and thus to help produce predictable results on important dimensions.	To create leadership processes, and thus to help produce changes needed to cope with a changing business environment.
Number	Usually 10-20% of the total jobs in an organization. In general, the more complex the operation, the more managerial roles.	Can vary enormously: 1–50% of the total jobs in an organization depending upon how much the operation needs to change.
Content	So called "line–management jobs" deal with all three aspects of management (planning, organizing, and control) for some domain. "Staff–management jobs" sometimes deal with only a limited piece of the overall process (e.g., budgeting or executive compensation) within some domain. Overall size of jobs can vary greatly from big to small.	Can vary enormously. Some will focus on all aspects of the leadership process for some activity or organization. Others will focus on a single aspect of the process (e.g., direction setting, or even one aspect of direction setting). Overall size of jobs can vary greatly from big (L) to small (l).
Assignment	Roles tend to be assigned to people as a formal part of the management process itself. People with management roles can also have leadership roles that are bigger or smaller than their management jobs.	Roles tend to be assigned or assumed by people in a more informal way and tend to be more fluid or changing. People with leadership roles usually also have management roles.

roles, for the same general reasons. A close inspection of the NCR case bears this out. The reason that the leadership process did not grind to a halt when Adamson left Dundee was that, by the time he left, that process was being driven to a significant degree by others. These people had learned something from Adamson about leadership, and they had been encouraged by him to provide it. These individuals did not number just one or two; they included many, if not most, of his entire management organization. Compared to Adamson, what they did was modest. The roles they played were specialized and limited but, nonetheless, extremely important. Some of these individuals helped provide all aspects of leadership for some part of the organization—the final assembly area, for example; others focused on one aspect of the process—helping Adamson with alignment or motivation, for example. Without people succeeding in these modest roles, Adamson alone would probably not have been able to provide all the leadership needed as the organization at Dundee grew, as it introduced additional products, and as life there generally became more complex. Moreover, without these people, the momentum would have died when he left.

Leadership in a modest sense—i.e., leadership with a lower-case (little) "l"[9]—is far more prevalent and far more important than most people realize. Not flashy or dramatic, it rarely attracts much attention, and often goes unnoticed. But it can be found in all leadership stories. It was present not only at NCR, but also at American Express, SAS, Kodak, Mary Kay, and Kentucky Fried Chicken.

Many of the Great Performer stories at TRS, for example, are "little" acts of leadership. In these cases, something unforeseen happens, often in the nature of a crisis. A person steps into the situation, figures out which direction things need to move, communicates that successfully to a few other people whose help is needed, and then energizes himself/herself and the others to make something happen under difficult conditions. Observers tend not to label this "leadership" because the number of people involved is so small, because the vision is so modest, and because the individuals do not fit our stereotype of leaders. But by the standards set in Chapters 3 to 5, this most certainly is leadership—only of the "l" kind.

One can sometimes find this same sort of leadership on the factory floor at Kodak's Copy Products. Here one of the workers comes up with an idea about how something can be improved, communicates that vision to a supervisor and a few fellow workers, and then helps get them excited enough to make it happen. For the most part, the person does not think of himself as a leader; yet he provides "l" leadership.

Without a lot of people like this, Mary Kay could not exist. These are those "ordinary" women who work part-time as beauty consultants and try to build their own direct-selling organizations. It is no small chore to attract people, train them, help them to set realistic goals, and motivate them. Without leadership, this does not happen. Some of these individuals probably think this task is something that pertains only to Mary Kay herself, not to them. But what they provide is most certainly leadership, and it is collectively of enormous importance.

So ingrained in our thinking is the traditional leader-follower model, that many people have difficulty imagining even two leaders in any one specific story. Yet for the same reason that it is possible to have 4 leadership roles in one case, it is possible to have 40 or 400. The Decworld '87 story provides a good example.[10]

Decworld '87, the creation of the Digital Equipment Corporation, took place in Boston during the first two weeks of September 1987. It was an exhibition for the firm's customers of Digital's products and people. By most standards, like the ARCO restructuring and the NCR ATM case, it was a real home run. But even more so than in those other two stories, virtually every knowledgeable source agrees that success here was the product of a large number of individuals helping to provide leadership.

Between September 1 and 11, 1987, no less than 32,000 people, representing 10,000 Digital accounts, came to Boston's World Trade Center for a two-and-a-half day tour of Decworld. During their stay, visitors saw a gigantic display of what Digital products could do for them. They attended lectures on computing and related subjects, choosing from a schedule that included 125 possibilities. They met Digital executives and had the opportunity to talk to their peers from other firms at a variety of social events—some hosted aboard the QE2 ocean liner or the Starship Oceanic, both of which were anchored next to the World Trade Center and used as floating hotels during this entire event. The visitors had dozens of opportunities to see new products, hear new ideas, ask questions and learn. Most left Boston extremely impressed.

Successful exhibitions of people and products are not at all unusual; firms have them all the time. What is unusual here was the scale of that event; Decworld '87 was the largest such exhibition ever put on by a single corporation, probably the largest by far. By many measures, it was also the most successful exhibition of its kind.

The free publicity alone, which was worldwide and often triggered by the two huge ocean liners, was worth tens (and probably even hundreds) of millions of dollars. Relationships were developed or strengthened with thousands of customers who controlled many billions of dollars worth of computer budgets. In terms of short-term business, in the three-and-a-half months following Decworld '87, Digital identified over $2 billion worth of new business in which the exhibition was mentioned as a contributing factor.

What is so extraordinary about the whole story is not, however, any of these statistics; it is that most large corporations would not even dream of trying something like this, because they could not imagine how it could be done: getting 25,000 employees, all of whom still had to perform their regular jobs, to put on a brilliantly conceived and superbly executed special event.

Yet, Digital people did it. They created and implemented a personalized campaign to get thousands of individuals to take time from their busy schedules to come to this event. They built a gigantic exhibit with $30 million worth of equipment organized into displays, by industry, so customers could clearly see what Digital could do for them. They created their own special closed-circuit television network with four anchors from local stations, and offered guests relevant programming in their hotels from 6:00 A.M. to 11:00 P.M. each day. They designed and implemented hundreds of special events for specific industries or major customers. They handled a logistical nightmare, which included serving 10,000 lunches a day. And they did all this with remarkably few mistakes, with a zest and style that impressed nearly everyone.

The leadership challenge of creating the various parts of this event, and the management challenge of seeing that it happened on time and on budget, were monumental. Yet these challenges were met—not by a single individual, nor by a small group of people like Cook and Arnault, but by a huge group of middle-level managers and professionals, most of whom played limited, but nevertheless important, roles.

At the center of this group were two teams of people, totalling about forty individuals. These teams provided much of the global leadership and management for the event. They worked with CEO Ken Olsen and Digital's top management to develop the basic concept for Decworld '87. They communicated that direction to the rest of the firm. They established overall timetables, a budget, and a structure for getting things done. They met regularly as the event got closer and closer to make sure things were on track, and to build up the enthusiasm that would be needed to make this all happen.

Both of these teams were headed by Dallas Kirk, the only Digital employee who was assigned full-time to Decworld. A former marketing manager for the electronics industry marketing group, Kirk, more than any other single individual, played the role of visible leader and head cheerleader. In doing so he worked very closely with Carmen Coletta. A financial manager from one of the marketing units, Coletta was officially in charge of finances for Decworld, but he also played Mr. Manager to Kirk's Mr. Leader. Using the budget as both a planning and control tool, Coletta organized the effort to establish targets and timetables, and to keep things on track. As a team, Kirk and Coletta provided a degree of strong leadership and management that neither of them could have given separately (see Exhibit 6.2).

Others in this central group included Janet Shipman, Craig Zamzow, Elizabeth Strong, and Kent St. Vrain. Shipman was responsible for

Exhibit 6.2　*Teamwork at Decworld '87*

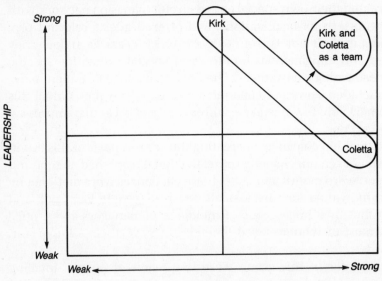

By working closely together, Kirk and Coletta provided a degree of
management and leadership that neither could have done separately.

developing and producing all the communication vehicles—including programs, invitations, signs, posters, the television network—as well as the overall visual look of the event. Zamzow was in charge of the display floor. His job was to turn Boston's World Trade Center into one gigantic interconnected set of multimillion dollar computer displays. Strong had responsibility for events. This required designing and implementing over 1,000 different activities, ranging from cerebral seminars to New England clambakes. And St. Vrain handled the invitation, registration, and housing of all the guests.

One step away from this center was a much larger group, 3,500 or so, who helped Shipman, Zamzow, Strong, and others. These individuals either managed or provided leadership for some specific part of the overall event—the demonstrations created for customers in one particular industry, for example. Assisting them were over 11,000 other Digital employees, who designed the various demonstrations, physically built and tested the systems, trained others to give demonstrations, and did hundreds of related activities.

Finally there were over 10,000 people who were physically present at Decworld for some period of time: running demos, giving speeches, handing out programs, having business meetings with customers, or trying to direct and motivate people doing these and other jobs. Most of those people carried out individual contributor assignments. But a sizable number of them were also asked either to manage some discrete event, to provide some leadership on a specific activity, or to do both.

In total, a huge number of people, in one form or another, helped provide some of the leadership and/or the management which this exhibition demanded in great quantity. Even more so than was seen in the ARCO case, they did this in a multitude of relatively small roles. This leadership with a lower-case (little) "l" may have been pretty modest in the case of many specific individuals, but collectively it was extraordinarily powerful. And it was at the very heart of the success of this event.

Among U.S. firms its size—1988 revenues of $11.5 billion—Digital is very unusual in its capacity to elicit leadership from significant numbers of middle-level managers and professionals. But compared to the most successful large firms in the world over the past twenty years, it is not at all unusual in this respect.

Many of those firms, the most successful worldwide, are from Japan. They include Sumitomo (banking), Matsushita (consumer electronics), Toyota (cars and trucks), Nomura (securities), Canon (copiers), and many others. When Americans think of the Japanese, they rarely think of leadership. Yet those corporations, in their culturally distinct way, have done a brilliant job at both management and leadership. The evidence of this is very clear, both in terms of results (consistently meeting the expectations of customers, bankers, etc., while also aggressively changing to meet new conditions) and in terms of factors that produce those results (good plans, organization, and controls coupled with a clear sense of direction, alignment to that direction, and highly motivated people). But they have achieved all this, not in the traditional American or European manner which often stresses a strong John Wayne-like figure at the top, but in a way that looks much more like Digital's.

Highly successful Japanese corporations frequently have exceptional individuals as CEOs. But a large part of the leadership in these firms comes from groups more than from individuals, and the groups are usually at middle levels. Hundreds of people play some role, yet often so modest that when one looks at single individuals, one rarely sees anything that resembles Western-style leadership. But leadership it is, and as a collectivity, it has helped firms adjust brilliantly to oil crises, yen/dollar crises, protective trade legislation, and much more—crises that would absolutely devastate many large corporations in the United States and Europe.

7

Thick Informal Networks

L eadership from multiple sources in a single situation does not have to converge; to the contrary, it can easily conflict. In extreme cases, the conflict can be disastrous; strong-willed individuals with competing visions can create a war-like atmosphere which squanders resources, accomplishes little, and exhausts everyone.

For multiple leadership roles to work together, something must coordinate the actions of people in those roles. In particular, a mechanism is needed to help link emerging visions together so they harmonize instead of compete. This can be most difficult to accomplish, but it is possible; consider the cases at ARCO and Digital. The key, however, is not the sort of thing that coordinates management roles. It is something quite different, something more suited to the character and function of leadership.

We take it for granted, more or less, that it is possible to have multiple people helping with a managerial process as long as their roles are a part of an intelligent formal structure which explicitly defines managerial roles and links them in a chain of command. Such a structure helps coordinate people both by reducing conflict and by resolving conflict in sensible ways. Job descriptions that are relatively unambiguous and do not overlap much help achieve the former; they reduce conflict, for example, by minimizing the chances of a territorial dispute. The chain of command helps achieve the latter by providing a mechanism that can resolve disputes; no matter which roles are in conflict, in a chain of command there is always someone hierarchically linked to those roles who can provide the needed coordination. Just as importantly, both job descriptions and the chain of command can, through the planning process, help produce a totally integrated set of plans which, in a sense, resolves conflict even before it occurs and becomes disruptive.[1]

It is tempting to assume that these same mechanisms, or some slight variation, can coordinate leadership roles. But they cannot, and for reasons that follow directly from the inherent differences between management and leadership.

Once again, much of this has to do with routine activities versus non-routine ones, or in a broader sense, with stability versus change. Formal structure handles routine extremely well. It does not deal with the novel and unexpected events associated with change nearly as well, and for a very simple reason. When things change a lot, it is not possible to define jobs in unambiguous and non-overlapping ways. Sometimes it is not even possible to know what jobs will be needed in the future. As a result, a great deal more conflict is generated and a lot more has to be actively resolved. Beyond a certain point, this overwhelms the hierarchy's capacity to deal with this sort of situation. People at the highest levels in the structure end up spending more and more time trying to cope with increasingly rancorous disputes. Decision making becomes slower and slower. Tension grows. Eventually the system collapses.[2]

When leadership roles are coordinated well, it is with something that is more flexible and adaptive than formal structure, and is therefore more able to deal with non-routine and with change. That something is more informal than formal, and is more spider web-like than hierarchical.[3]

At both ARCO and Digital, there were a multitude of good working relationships among people in the various specialized leadership roles. These individuals often knew and respected each other. In some cases they had worked together for decades and were very close personally. They shared common values which helped bind them together. In some cases, they even shared similar world views.

These thick networks of informal relationships help coordinate leadership activities in much the same way as formal structure coordinates managerial activities. The key difference is that thick informal networks can deal with the greater coordinating demands associated with non-routine activities and change. The multitude of communication channels and the trust among the individuals con-

nected by those channels allow for an ongoing process of accommodation and adaptation regarding who will play what role. When conflicts arise between roles, those same relationships among parties
with shared values help resolve the conflicts. Perhaps most important, this process of dialogue and accommodation can produce visions
which are linked and compatible instead of remote and competitive.
All of this requires a great deal more communication than is needed
to coordinate managerial roles, but unlike formal structure, thick informal networks can handle that communication (see Exhibit 7.1).

The importance of linked visions cannot be overstated. Without
them, the dialogue and accommodation needed to coordinate every-
day actions would eventually overwhelm the capabilities of even the
strongest informal network. With interlocked visions, people in specialized leadership roles can act quite independently, yet without constant conflict with others. In the Kentucky Fried Chicken story, for
example, at least a dozen people had to develop visions for their particular pieces of the project. Yet because these visions were consistent
with Dick Mayer's overall concept, and because inconsistencies
among them were worked out, these individuals were able to proceed
with some autonomy, and the whole project was able to move with
unusual speed.

Thick networks can even help coordinate leadership and manage-

Exhibit 7.1 *Coordinating Management Roles vs. Leadership Roles*

	Multiple Management Roles	Multiple Leadership Roles
Primary coordinating mechanisms	Formal structure (job descriptions and chain of command) and integrated plans.	Thick informal networks (good working relationships among many people who share certain values) and overlapping visions.
Process by which mechanisms work	Job descriptions specify responsibilities and authority and reduce conflict by minimizing overlap between jobs. Chains of command link all jobs, and thus provide a vehicle for resolving conflict. These same mechanisms, when applied to the planning process, create an integrated set of plans, which eliminate future conflict.	The multitude of good communication channels and trust among people in thick informal networks allow for an ongoing process of accommodation and adaptation regarding who plays what role, and regarding conflict among roles. Those channels also help produce visions that are linked and compatible instead of remote and competitive.

ment roles when they are performed by different people, as in the case of Dallas Kirk and Carmen Coletta at Digital.

Of course, informal relations of some sort exist in all corporations. But all too often these networks are either very thin—some people are well connected but most are not—or they are highly fragmented—a tight network exists inside the marketing group and inside R&D but not across the two departments. Such networks do not support multiple leadership initiatives well.

Because of all this, thick informal networks are vitally important to leadership, and one finds them wherever multiple leadership initiatives work in harmony. They were present at Dundee. They were very much a part of the American Express story. The successes at Kodak and Kentucky Fried Chicken depended upon them. The same can be said of all the best Japanese corporations. So important is the network, that if it does not exist or is inadequate, its creation has to be the focus of activity early in a major leadership initiative.

The story of Procter & Gamble's paper products division in the mid-1980s is a good example of a business turnaround produced by multiple leadership initiatives in a setting that did not, at first, include an adequate informal network.[4]

Paper products at Procter & Gamble is made up of well-known brands like Bounty (paper towels), Pampers (disposable diapers), and Charmin (bathroom tissue). The division is a key revenue producer among P&G's food, soap, health, and beauty care businesses.

Although P&G is over 150 years old, the paper products division was only started in 1956 with the acquisition of the Charmin Paper Company. Charmin had one product, bathroom tissue, which was sold regionally in the United States. P&G moved very aggressively to grow this business, and was enormously successful over a period of twenty years. The firm used a three-pronged approach. Product development expertise was utilized to extend the range of the product line; disposable diapers, for example, were introduced in 1961. New manufacturing technologies were developed to produce high-quality paper goods at a low cost. Then, marketing and sales expertise was used to expand geographically the distribution of products—to national markets and then international.

At first, P&G had little competition for these innovative, high-quality, reasonably priced, and well-marketed consumer goods. By the late 1970s, that had changed. Huggies by Kimberly Clark made important inroads into Pampers' market share. Northern bathroom tissue and Brawny paper towels, both produced by James River, became more and more successful. The Scott Paper Company developed a more aggressive and effective stand. Inexpensive private labels produced by firms like Georgia-Pacific, Weyerhaeuser, and Fort Howard, began to consume additional market share. In combination, these new competitive thrusts hurt P&G, and hurt them badly; industry analysts estimate that P&G's market share for disposable diapers fell from 75 percent in the mid-1970s to 52 percent in 1984.[5]

When senior management realized the magnitude of the problem, they began assigning people to the paper products division who they felt could help produce a turnaround. Chief among these new people was Richard Nicolosi.

In April 1984, Nicolosi came to paper products as the associate general manager. After three years in P&G's smaller and faster-moving soft drink business, he found an organization that seemed very functionally oriented and centralized. The focus was internal, on functional goals and projects. Almost all information about customers came through highly quantitative market research. The technical people were rewarded for cost savings, the commercial people focused on volume and share, and the two were nearly at war with each other.

During the late summer of 1984, top management announced that Nicolosi would become the head of paper products in October. By August, he was effectively running the division. His first major move was made in September, when for three days, he and his eleven direct reports met off-site. "I had to make it very clear," Nicolosi later reported, "that the rules of the game had changed."

It was a difficult meeting; the twelve individuals were not used to working as a group. Nevertheless, with the help of a person skilled in team building, they initiated a dialogue, started to improve their working relationships, and began the formulation of a new direction for the division.

The new direction was one that included a much greater stress on teamwork; the strategy of using groups of people to manage the organization and specific products was pushed by Nicolosi and accepted by most of the others. So was the idea that the division needed to become much more creative and market driven, instead of just trying to be a low-cost producer. They also discussed the need to move more quickly with innovations, the notion of focusing more on customers and total quality, and the concept that business performance should be their objective, not endless analyses and functional projects.

In October, these same twelve people designated themselves as the paper division "Board" and began meeting monthly. Six months later, these meetings increased in frequency to weekly. During this period, Board members who were obviously having difficulty fitting in with the group and adjusting to the new direction found assignments in other parts of P&G.

In November, the Board established "category teams" to manage their major groups of brands (e.g., diapers, tissues, towels). Nicolosi and a few others spent many hours explaining to the departments and the new teams their emerging vision of how the division would now operate, and the role of these teams. Wendy Williams[6] developed a workshop to help category-team members think about their new jobs in terms of leadership. At the same time, Nicolosi and his Board started pushing responsibility down to these category teams and urging them to be bold. "Shun the incremental," he would say, "and go for the leap." To encourage creative thinking, Nicolosi also started sending countless notes to people. "Have you considered this?" "What about this idea?"

In December, Nicolosi selectively involved himself in more detail in certain activities. He personally met with the advertising agency and got to know key creative people. He asked the marketing manager of diapers, Peter Hemme, to report directly to him, eliminating a layer in the hierarchy. He talked more to the people who were working on two new development projects for products that would eventually be known as Always Plus and Ultra Pampers.

In January 1985, the Board announced the following new organizational structure that included not only category teams, but also new brand business teams:

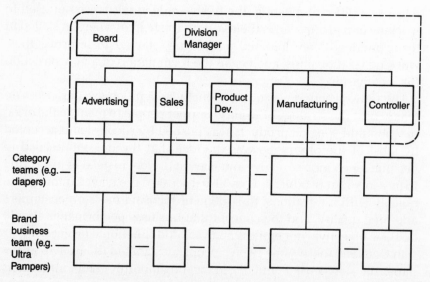

At first there was considerable confusion about how this structure would work. But there also was a good deal of excitement. To help people think about their roles in the new structure, a couple of individuals on the Board began to talk much less about managing and much more about leading.

By April, with strong encouragement from Board members, manufacturing and engineering started focusing on "Total Quality." People like Steve Brunner and Paul Kissling looked for systemic ways to make the operation more productive and profitable.

In May, with a clearer sense of the direction needed for the division, the Board planned in great detail a major event for June 4 to communicate that vision to as many people as possible. On that day, all the Cincinnati-based personnel in paper plus sales district managers and paper plant managers, several thousand people in total, met in the local Masonic Temple. Nicolosi talked passionately about the changing competitive environment and the need for all of them to change. Board members described their vision of a division that achieves consistent volume and profit growth by being the world's number one marketer of superior value paper and disposable products to the consumer, an organization that achieves that end by providing the best possible environment for human growth, contribution, and productivity, that runs the business with a total quality approach, that fosters creativity and innovation, that has a superior understanding of the consumer and the competition, that works in collaborative teams with short and open lines of communication, and in which "each of us is a leader." This was followed by a brief communique from each category-team leader who reinforced the message. Next came a broadcast-quality video that starred some of these same people singing and dancing.

After the video, everyone was ushered onto a riverboat which proceeded to cruise up the Ohio River to Coney Island Amusement Park. At the park, there were more speeches, a sit-down dinner, another video on "the new direction," and a brass band for everyone's amusement. The evening ended with fireworks. More than one long-tenured P&G employee was heard saying, "I've worked for this company for a lot of years, and I've never seen anything quite like this before."

The entire June 4 affair was videotaped. An edited version was sent to all sales offices and plants, and virtually all of the division's employees who were not at the event saw the videotape.

After this extravaganza, the departments and category teams began to develop their own vision and strategy statements. One department took seventy people off-site for two days, and another involved everyone "down through the secretaries." These meetings were sometimes difficult, but not nearly as contentious as the first off-site meeting of the Board held the previous September. By now a combination of the new structure and divisional vision, both of which encouraged teamwork, together with selective personnel changes, training in teamwork, and lots of team-building meetings all conspired to create many more healthy working relationships within and across departments.

To reinforce these direction-setting actions and encourage them, members of the Board spent endless hours talking about the overall direction and the progress they were making, all with great enthusiasm. Nicolosi traveled two days a week to plants and sales offices. He wanted everyone to see his personal conviction and commitment to the changes that were being made. Many people found his enthusiasm to be infectious.

In August, the Board began looking for some "early wins" that could give the new visions credibility and help motivate everyone. They chose to focus first on the pricing and promotion structure for tissues and towels. The approach was simple: Forget maximizing profit margins for now, go for share; when the business starts growing, the focus can shift to getting margins up. They also began focusing more time on two new products: Always Plus and Ultra Pampers. Each of these investments paid off handsomely.

Late that same year, the management of the paper division began planning a process by which people new to the organization could be quickly introduced to their changed orientation. Starting in January 1986, all new managers were brought to Cincinnati for three-and-a-half days during which they met other divisional employees, and heard about the business direction.

To keep old employees on track, Nicolosi began rewarding each and every achievement with personal notes, flowers, and plaques, in addition to the usual promotions and raises. Other senior executives did the same, and by midyear almost everyone was talking about the "cultural change" at paper. A report written during the summer of 1986 reported "better communication, collaboration, and trust, and more teamwork" (i.e., a much thicker informal network of relationships). It also reported "more focus and direction, more and better strategies, better alignment, improved morale and better, faster, and more initiatives" (i.e., more leadership from multiple sources).

By then, leadership was bubbling up all over the division.

P&G development engineers had known about AGM (absorbent gel-ling material) for years. When three Japanese companies found a way to make this substance for a third of what it had previously cost, P&G engineers decided to try to use it to make a diaper. Its capacity to absorb twenty-eight times its weight in water would, at least in theory, help make a much thinner, better fitting, and better performing product.

The project was launched in 1983; the development organization created a successful diaper, and in October 1984 manufacturing produced a first batch. A number of people on the paper products Board liked the product concept because it was a leap forward. When Jay Curry was appointed brand manager, he was given no other responsibilities to divert his attention from this important innovation.

The new product offered two obvious marketing challenges. First, consumers had been taught to believe that thicker was better for diapers. Second, chemicals of any kind next to the human body, much less a baby's body, were thought to be off limits. Some people felt these two red flags dictated a slow approach and much caution. But all the people working on the AGM project were urged to move ahead and move ahead quickly. When they did, the Board supported their initiatives.

To overcome the concern about chemicals, the AGM team sponsored clinical studies of the product in use, and collected endorsement after endorsement from doctors—something that had never been done before in disposable diaper marketing. To deal with the thicker-is-better problem, they worked on advertising and decided to send samples directly to consumers' homes at the time of national expansion—again, something that had never been done before in the diaper business.

In September 1985, the brand team chose a name for the product, despite conventional wisdom that held you never use a word like "ultra" on a brand because it somehow denigrates the regular product. The team ignored traditional thinking and called the AGM product "Ultra Pampers."

A test market was run in October 1985, and national expansion began the following February. Instead of a traditional slow and methodical roll-out, the product was offered nearly everywhere from the very beginning. The idea, again untraditional, was to surprise the competition.

The results were impressive; with the aid of this new product, the Pampers line went from a 40 percent share to 58 percent, and its profitability went from break-even to substantially positive. The once sleepy paper products division scored a major victory.

At the same time that P&G was making a comeback in a category in which it had been traditionally very strong, the firm also was making major inroads in a new sector: catamenial pads.

Seventy-five percent of women experience some form of failure, during their period, from the pads or tampons they use for protection. With this in mind, Joe Makey in product development, Tony Jones in manufacturing, and a few others at P&G decided to try to create a new product that was not just an incremental protection improvement—but something that was more revolutionary.

P&G development engineers ran studies to find what caused sanitary products to fail. They discovered that most of the problem was due to area coverage; pads are two inches wide, but panty crotches are three inches wide. After much experimentation and effort, they found a way to add extra area coverage and reduce the failure rate from 75 percent to 25 percent. The product, eventually called Always Plus, was odd looking; but in terms of performance, it was a leap forward.

Early in 1984, a brand group was assigned to manage the product. Betsy Frye was made brand manager. A passionate and visionary individual, she believed strongly in the concept and its potential. But she quickly identified a problem with selling it—communicating what this odd-looking product was, what it did, and how to use it.

The Board liked Always Plus from the beginning; it clearly fit their emerging vision of the kind of product they wanted to market. They made this clear to Frye, and energetically supported her efforts.

The initial test market for Always Plus was Columbus, Ohio, in February 1985. The results were disappointing. Historically, a disappointing test market would slow or even kill a new product. The Board urged the brand team not to let this happen, but to use the experience as something to learn from. Frye accepted the challenge and did just that.

Over a two- to three-month period, Betsy Frye convinced the advertising agency that the ads needed to be changed, and had to be more explicit if consumers were to understand the product. This would mean actually showing underwear and using the word "panties" in television spots—something that had never been done before. After much discussion, the agency followed Frye's lead. The new advertising was tried in a second test market, this time in Phoenix in July 1985. The results were much better.

During the fall of that year, the team geared up for national expansion. Convention dictated that they use the same ads and other marketing devices in national expansion as were used in the successful test market. But between the summer of 1985 and the spring of 1986, the agency developed yet another ad. Many who saw it thought the new ad was better. Nicolosi was asked for his opinion. "Forget the rules," he said, "and do what is right."

In a roll-out that began in May 1986, the new ads were used. The results started strong and then grew even stronger. The Always product line went from a negative to break-even profit position up to a substantial profit, and at a speed much faster than expected. Always Plus took the brand from second or third place to nearly a tie for first in its category. Overall, it was another major victory.

Most innovative initiatives during this period came from people dealing with new products like Ultra Pampers and Always Plus. But not all. Some thrusts were more oriented toward a functional area, and some literally came from the bottom of the hierarchy. In the spring of 1986, a few of the division's secretaries, feeling empowered by the new culture, developed a Secretaries Network. This association established three subcommittees: one on the secretary of the future, one on training, and one on rewards and recognition. The training committee, for example, worked with the personnel function to create a development seminar for secretaries; the first was held in the fall of 1986. The network sponsored a meeting in April 1987 to "foster better communication and trust among support staff" which was attended by 187 secretaries. Network subcommittees also helped write a training and reference manual for secretaries, and launched a regular newsletter called "The Secretarial Agenda." Echoing the sentiments of many of her peers, one paper products secretary said: "I didn't see why we can't also contribute to the division's new direction."

The year 1987 saw more new product successes; Luvs Delux was introduced in May and within only a few months the market share for the overall brand grew to 150 percent of its previous level. Accomplishments like this were trumpeted in a twelve-page pamphlet sent to all divisional employees in the summer of that year. Called "A Celebration of Progress," this booklet started with a letter from Nicolosi: "On June 4, 1985, we began a journey to excellence . . . . " It then included dozens of comments by people, along with their pictures, regarding what they have done to help make the vision a reality; described the new "paper division operational approach"; and talked about the 1987 version of their vision, mission, and strategies. Finally, the booklet showed pictures of people on the Board, and concluded with a personal message from Nicolosi about his beliefs and values.

The bottom line, according to interviews conducted in late 1987, was: "We have successfully made some necessary alterations in a deeply embedded culture—no small accomplishment even by itself— and these changes are having a big impact. Versus a few years ago, what has happened in all our categories is that we are generally here in the marketplace ahead of the competition with new ideas." Economic results, as of the end of 1988, looked like this: Revenues were up 40 percent over a four-year period. Profits were up 66 percent. And this happened despite the fact that the competition continued to get tougher.

Really strong competition almost always creates continuous change in an industry, as firms struggle again and again to gain some advantage. If an individual business is at all complex—à la the paper division at P&G—it will have to change in thousands of ways to adapt to those conditions, and that magnitude of change demands leadership efforts initiated by a multitude of people. Nothing less will work.

That does not mean that single individuals are not important. Nicolosi was obviously central to this story. But it took more than one person to set the division on a new course, align people to it, and inspire them to action. It required more than one strong executive to create the thick informal networks needed to support multiple leadership initiatives: by creating the Board and getting it to become a model of teamwork, by getting groups of people throughout the division to develop visions and strategies, by creating a new organizational structure that forced more teamwork, by communicating endlessly the new division-level vision, by replacing key people who were having trouble fitting in, and by creating the type of group celebration held in June 1985. It took more than one person to encourage people to lead, and to support their efforts, especially when those individuals came under attack from entrenched bureaucratic factions.

In the final analysis, it was leadership from all those on the Board, and then from dozens of other people, that produced the turnaround. Nothing less would have worked.

IV

The Origins
of Leadership

8

Heredity and Childhood

It is generally accepted today that management can largely be taught to adults either in school or on the job. It is also widely believed that leadership is much more difficult to teach, but consensus on its exact origin stops there. Some people think that genes and early life experiences create leaders. Others point to events later in life. Indeed, few questions have caused more heated debate over the years than: Are leaders born or made?

It is not possible to say with certainty or precision much about the roots of leadership. Nevertheless, an assessment of the current state of our knowledge in this area is important because any attempt to increase the amount of leadership in organizations must be based on some assumptions about the role of heredity and childhood. The better the assumptions, the more successful these efforts will be.

In the late 1970s, I studied in some considerable depth a group of successful executives who were in jobs like Adamson's, Gerstner's, and Mayer's,[1] and worked for nine different corporations in a wide variety of industries. Over a two-year period, each executive was observed in his work setting at some length, as well as interviewed and tested. Their colleagues were also interviewed, and relevant company documents were obtained.

Although there was a great deal of diversity in terms of what these executives did and how they did it, there were also some fundamental similarities, especially among the ones who appeared to be performing their jobs most effectively. Specifically, they created agendas for themselves made up of loosely connected sets of short-term plans, medium-term strategies, and long-term visions. They each built resource networks that could accomplish these agendas by staffing and structuring the jobs reporting to them, by communicating their plans and visions to people, and by establishing cooperative relationships with a broad range of individuals whose help they might need. They then actively sought to influence people in those networks when necessary to assure the achievement of their agendas, and did so in a wide variety of ways, sometimes trying to control people and activities, sometimes attempting to inspire others to new heights of performance. Overall, this behavior was extremely complex and, as has been reported in other in-depth studies of executives at work,[2] did not look much like traditional management.

What these executives were doing, employing the language of this book, was a combination of management, leadership, and still other things (chief among which was the development of sources of power that could help them manage, lead, and get promoted). But all of these various aspects of behavior were highly intertwined. They did not manage for fifteen minutes and then lead for half-an-hour. Instead, in the course of a single, five-minute conversation, they might try to see if some activity was proceeding as planned (a control part of management), gather information that was relevant to their emerging vision (the direction-setting part of leadership), promise to do someone a favor (an aspect of power development), and agree on a series of steps for accomplishing some objective (the planning part of management). As a result, to the observer, what they were doing did not look much like management or any other recognizable activity. The managers themselves even found their own behavior difficult to describe and explain.

Nevertheless, although this behavior was complex, when one took into account the nature of their jobs and the demands placed on them, it basically made sense. Again employing the language of this book, they were being asked to produce consistent short-term results to satisfy key constituencies, and so they managed. They were also being asked to help their organizations adapt to changing competition, technology, and markets, and so they led. But their jobs did not automatically give them the power to lead or manage effectively, especially the former, so they built and maintained personal power bases. Because doing all this could consume 100 or more hours a week, they found efficient ways to accomplish multiple purposes in single activities or interactions; as a result, various aspects of management, leadership, and power development behavior became highly intertwined.

An analysis of why they were able to do all this well uncovered a significant number of seemingly relevant personal characteristics, many of which appear to have helped them lead.[3] For example, almost all of them had a set of interpersonal skills and interests which allowed them to relate to a broad range of people in their business contexts; these attributes helped them gather information in the direction-setting aspect of leadership, communicate effectively in aligning people to that direction, and stress the right themes in their efforts to energize individuals.

Of the characteristics they shared, approximately one-third probably have roots in heredity or early life experiences. A typical example would be above-average intelligence, an asset that appears to be particularly helpful in the direction-setting aspect of leadership in complex settings. The rest of the shared characteristics are more obviously associated with experiences that come after puberty. A typical example would be a strong track record that establishes one's credibility, and thus helps the aligning aspect of leadership.

This study is interesting because an analysis of the leadership processes described in Chapters 3 through 5, and of the people involved in these processes in the stories recorded in this book, reveals something similar. A list of fifteen to twenty attributes seem to be shared by the Adamson's and Gerstner's and Nicolosi's of the world, and four of these characteristics are probably fixed or largely set early in life.

Perhaps the most obvious of the characteristics that are established before puberty is one relating to drive, ambition, or energy level. People who provide effective leadership in "L" roles always seem to have above-average energy levels, often much above average. They appear to thrive on achieving something important and being in a position of influencing others to achieve. This inner drive is often associated with high personal standards, a certain dissatisfaction with the status quo, and a tendency to push for continuing improvements (what the Japanese call "Kaizen"). Observers often sense this restless ambition after being with people like Jim Adamson or Jan Carlzon for only a short period of time. Even if it is not obvious on the surface, individuals who know these people well always talk about this attribute.[4]

A strong internal drive to achieve and succeed is probably essential here, simply because leadership in jobs such as Carlzon's can be absolutely exhausting. The hours are long. The problems can be huge. Yet it takes a sustained effort for years in those jobs to accomplish the kinds of changes associated with leadership. It is difficult to imagine people with less than a high level of internal drive handling the hours and the problems over such a long period of time.

Energy level can be affected by adult experiences. Reading Lee Iacocca's first book,[5] one cannot help but feel that a part of his drive to make Chrysler succeed was fueled by his being fired by Henry Ford II. Nevertheless, for most people most of the time, internal motivation is probably established early in life. People who knew Lou Gerstner, for example, either when he was a child or a young man, regularly comment on his determination and drive even then. Genes may play some role in this, but for certain a child's relationships are very important: to mother, father, and other close figures.

Some form of intelligence or intellectual skill seems to be a second relevant attribute. The nature of intelligence is a controversial issue today. As a result, it is not possible to say much here except that people who provide effective leadership in big jobs appear to be always above average in some basic form of intelligence, although they rarely seem to be geniuses. Occasionally this is obvious; Mayer and Gerstner have minds that quickly impress. Sometimes this is more subtle; Mary Kay hides her considerable IQ under Southern lace.

Intellectual skills and abilities are probably especially important to direction setting. Assimilating a huge quantity of diverse information and sensing relevant patterns in that information is a task of considerable cognitive complexity.[6]

This attribute is certainly developed by education in childhood, but it undoubtedly has some biological roots, which means heredity and pre-natal care. It is an unusual person who appears to have below-average intelligence at age ten and then above-average at age forty (by all reasonable measures, not just an IQ test or one set of school grades).

Mental or emotional health seems to be yet another important attribute. People like Bob Crandall and Lod Cook appear to carry a minimum of "psychological baggage" and rarely if ever seem narcissistic, paranoid, or highly insecure.[7] This allows them to interact with the world, and particularly with people, with a minimum of distortions or problems. In a sense, emotional health is probably a base upon which so-called interpersonal skills grow. When that base is missing or weak, those kind of skills seem to have difficulty emerging in later years.

This trait is probably very useful in all aspects of the leadership process, because all three parts have an interpersonal component.[8] But in particular, it must certainly help a great deal in motivating people, where an accurate reading of feelings and values is important. And a lack of distortion must be essential in direction setting; some of the most terrifying leaders throughout history seem to have let their deep emotional problems create tragic visions.

Mental health has some roots in biology; psychosis has been related to chemical imbalances that may be inherited. It also involves early life experiences; a great deal of Freud's pioneering work demonstrated how certain kinds of events in childhood create neurotic defensive routines which can persist throughout life.

Integrity seems to be another important attribute, for at least two reasons. Many people are remarkably capable in assessing whether a person values others and their well-being; they just watch what the person does and what impact that has. Someone whose integrity is questioned by others will, in particular, have great difficulty with alignment. People will not believe what he or she says, and they will be very reluctant to follow his or her lead.

Integrity also contributes to good direction setting, especially for individuals with a lot of drive. Ambitious and driven people whose integrity is not strong will often select a course which allows for movement, achievement, and some glory, but which eventually fails because it does not satisfy the legitimate needs of the constituencies involved. Great drive has a dark side, and without integrity, it can pervert leadership.

Integrity is influenced by major events in adulthood; people and circumstances can corrupt an individual. But again, the roots of this attribute, like the other three, probably go back to early life. The values held and/or expressed by significant adults are particularly important: mother, father, even elementary school teachers.

Taken together, the four attributes—intelligence, drive, mental health, and integrity, or some slight variation on these themes—seem to define some minimum requirements for leadership in big jobs. Having more of each does not necessarily help; above a certain level, twice the intelligence or mental health does not seem to produce better leadership. But if any of the four are missing to some minimum degree, effective leadership may be undermined (see Exhibit 8.1).

There may be still more relevant attributes, but surely not many. Overall it is a very short list, much shorter than some people would expect. It is also a remarkably mundane list. There is certainly noth-

Exhibit 8.1 *Heredity, Childhood, and Leadership in Big Jobs*

Traits From Heredity or Childhood	Effect on Leadership in Big Jobs
Drive/energy level	Without a great deal of inner drive, the difficulties in producing change over a period of years tend to discourage people from leading.
Intelligence/intellectual skills	Without sufficient basic intelligence, it is often difficult to set the right direction in a complex environment.
Mental/emotional health	Without some minimum amount of mental/emotional health, all the interpersonal skills needed for leadership tend not to develop over time. The distortions caused by emotional problems can also create tragically flawed visions.
Integrity	Large numbers of people never follow individuals who, they believe, to be lacking in integrity, except for short periods of time. Also, highly driven individuals who lack integrity often establish a course that, if people do follow, will eventually lead to tragedy.

ing magical about any of the items in Exhibit 8.1. Missing from the list is the more mysterious element that many people would expect to find: a charismatic personality. Although some people who provide leadership in big jobs do have that magnetic personal appeal, many do not; of all the individuals named in this book, only one or two are highly charismatic.

Also missing from the list are a number of attributes which we often associate with heredity or childhood, but which are developed mostly in adults. A good example would be a propensity for risk-taking. There is no question that early life experiences shape our attitudes toward risk. But career experiences and organizational culture can have an even more profound effect; an adult who is punished by an employer every time he or she takes a risk, and/or is rewarded for very cautious behavior, will usually become averse to risk.

But despite the ordinariness of the key attributes, remarkably few people share all four. The world is full of smart people with emotional problems, mentally healthy people with only an average motivation level, people high in integrity who have average intelligence, and so on. Although it is difficult to estimate, it is quite possible that less than one in fifty people meet all four criteria.[9] If this is true, it confirms the commonsense notion that relatively few young adults have the potential to provide effective leadership in jobs as big as Carlzon's. But it does not confirm the leaders-are-born-not-made theory, because all leadership jobs are not like Carlzon's.

There are a multitude of different kinds of leadership roles in complex organizations. At one extreme, they are big and broad, like those played by Lou Gerstner and Dick Nicolosi. At the opposite extreme, they are small and very specialized, such as the ones played by Gerstner's Great Performers or some participants in Decworld. When the roles are big and broad, the requirements for playing them well are severe. As one moves toward the other end of that continuum, the requirements become more and more modest, as do the childhood or genetic roots of those requirements.

A middle-level manager at ARCO, who helped provide occasional leadership in making its West Coast refinery more efficient, did not need the personal assets possessed by current ARCO Chairman Lod Cook or past Chairman Robert Anderson. Depending upon the exact role this person played, he or she may not have needed nearly as much drive, or intelligence, or even emotional health. In a similar vein, the production worker at Kodak who provided "l" leadership once or twice a year did not need the attributes of the middle-level refinery manager.

If we think of leadership roles on a continuum, with the biggest jobs on one end and the smallest on the other, then perhaps only a percent or two of the population has the heredity and childhood experiences needed at the "big" end. That percentage grows as we move toward the "small" end, possibly reaching a high of well over 50 percent. In the middle of the continuum, perhaps in jobs like that refinery supervisor's, the percentage may be in the 10 to 30 percent range.

This brings us to the heart of much of the seemingly irreconcilable debate on "born versus made." People who argue that leaders are born tend to be thinking of leadership roles on the big end of the continuum. If we are correct in saying that less than 1 or 2 percent of the population has the attributes from heredity and childhood to play these roles well, then it is accurate to say that these people are born into circumstances linked to leadership potential while the vast majority of humanity is not. People who argue that leaders are made, more often than not, are thinking of smaller and more specialized roles. Again, if we are correct in saying that over half the population has the necessary heredity and childhood experiences to play modest roles, then it is accurate to say that such people are not born to leadership but come to it by later experiences and circumstances.

This is not the only reason why people disagree strongly about the origins of leadership. People on the "born" side of the argument tend to see virtually all relevant attributes as being formed early in life, while people who take the "made" side of the debate attribute the same traits to later life experiences. But the range of leadership roles creates at least as much confusion as do different assumptions about the origin of various attributes.

It is not possible to prove this interpretation. But it is possible to test the most general conclusions drawn here by looking at firms that seem to have more than average leadership in a wide variety of roles.

In 1986, I conducted a study of fifteen corporations that had reputations for doing a superior job of attracting and developing people with leadership potential.[10] This study is interesting, for our purposes here, because the findings are consistent with and reinforce the conclusions just drawn about the role of heredity and childhood experiences.

All but one of these firms had high-potential recruiting efforts, although some did not choose to call them that because of the elitist implications. Aimed at finding young people with the potential of some day performing well in moderately large- to large-leadership roles, these recruiting programs all shared two characteristics. First, they were very aggressive. The implicit assumption was that few people had the attributes they desired to hire, so, in a competitive labor market, they had to be aggressive and well organized to find such people. Second, each focused on the four attributes identified earlier in this chapter. Some labeled these traits as we have here; others used different names. But the general idea was the same.

Aggressive recruiting typically manifested itself in four ways. These firms usually identified good sources of people for them and then attempted to develop relationships with those labor markets. Hewlett-Packard, for example, was at the time of the study focusing its corporate recruiting efforts on thirty colleges and universities where it was, among other things, networking with key faculty and donating computer equipment. These firms asked high-level line managers to participate heavily in the recruiting effort. Even the chairmen at firms like General Mills and Merck were involved. When they found a person that was especially promising, these firms were sophisticated in knowing how to close the sale. At a minimum, they worked very diligently to convince people to accept offers. Most of these corporations also worked had to keep the recruiting standards high, even in decentralized environments. Morgan Guaranty, for example, brought all its high-potential recruits to a lengthy training program in New York which, among other things, allowed corporate officers to see if any of their offices were allowing standards to slip.

To attract people in a competitive labor market, almost all of these firms also worked at creating and maintaining a good work environment. Such an environment was relatively low in bureaucracy and politics, and relatively high in respect for competence, initiative, integrity, and human dignity.

Most of these firms did not have a clear written profile of what they were seeking in these recruiting efforts; nevertheless, if one talks to the senior officials involved, a common profile emerges. They look for people who are reasonably smart; grades, test scores, and an ability to think in an interview are all seen as indices. They look for people who are motivated; grades, extracurricular activities in school, and any kind of achievement against difficult odds are seen as relevant. They want people with integrity; anything in a person's record that might indicate a lack of this trait is seen as potentially important. Finally, they seek people who can relate well to others; this is labeled in many different ways, but the underlying issue is the absence of a history of interpersonal problems that seem to be caused by emotional difficulties.

These same firms did not spend as much time or as many resources in the rest of their recruiting, although on average, they invested more than most corporations. The traits sought in this general recruiting were considerably vaguer, or at least less generalizable, than those in high-potential recruiting. Mostly the focus was on technical factors needed to perform entry-level jobs (e.g., an engineering degree for an engineering job).[11] Nevertheless, especially in efforts aimed at people who might one day be in moderate-sized leadership roles, one hears many references to intelligence, initiative/motivation, interpersonal skills, and integrity.

People who believe in the overwhelming importance of heredity and childhood to leadership often employ the concept of charisma as the linking variable. The logic is straightforward. Charisma is the attri-

bute most important to being a good leader, especially a good motiva-
tor, and charisma is not something that is learned later in life; it
comes with genes and the early personality forming years.

This belief is important because it is often used to justify corporate
policies of benign neglect regarding the development of people's leadership potential. It is also employed by individuals, often uncon-
sciously, to rationalize a passive stance toward their own career
development.

There is no way to prove in a scientific sense, at least today,
whether this belief about charisma is right or wrong. But the following observations are highly suggestive. First, the majority of people
described in this book as leaders are not considered to be highly charismatic by most of the people who know them. Second, the one person most often identified as charismatic, Mary Kay, has some
interesting thoughts on the subject which do not support widespread
beliefs about that attribute.

Ask people why Mary Kay is such a good leader, and they often
refer very quickly to her charisma. Ask them why they think she is
charismatic, and they refer to how she speaks to groups of people and
how they respond to her; that is, they point to her naturally charismatic speaking style—something that, for sure, she was born with.
But ask Mary Kay about all this, and her response emphasizes something different. "People are often amazed at how I can talk about the
firm so naturally and spontaneously, without any notes. What they
don't realize is that it has taken me years to get to the point where I
can do this as well as I do. Oh, I'm sure I have some natural ability, but
that's only one part of it."

Charisma is not that important to effective leadership in complex
organizations. Even for people who are perceived as charismatic,
their experiences as adults often contribute to that sense of personal
magnetism.

9

Career Experiences

People do change after puberty, especially in their capacity to handle complex tasks and situations. Specific events rarely have much impact, although they can. But the accumulation of experiences over a decade or two is usually very influential. This is true in a general sense, but it is especially relevant with respect to leadership.

To do what Nicolosi, Mayer, and others like them have done requires much more than intelligence, drive, integrity, and emotional well-being. Effective direction setting demands a breadth of knowledge of relevant industries, an appreciation of the elements of sound business strategy, and a certain comfort with taking risks. Alignment requires a number of different communication skills, an understanding of the various groups of people to whom one is communicating, and credibility based on good working relationships and a sound track record. Motivating people demands a basic understanding of human nature, insight into the core values of the specific individuals with whom one works, and a certain amount of empathy. All of these attributes are developed, at least to some degree, after childhood. Individuals who are effective in relatively large leadership roles often share in common a number of experiences which appear to be extremely important in developing just these kinds of factors.[1]

Perhaps the most typical, and important, experience of this kind is real challenge early in a career. People like Carlzon and Cook almost always have had opportunities during their twenties and thirties to actually try to lead, to take a risk, and to learn from both triumphs and failures. Such learning seems to be essential in developing a wide range of leadership skills and perspectives. It also teaches people something about the difficulty of leadership, yet its potential in producing change. It helps them see that management techniques alone do not work when it comes to adapting organizations to shifting environments. It even provides people with insight into their own relative strengths and weaknesses pertaining to leadership.

Adamson got an opportunity of this sort in the Royal Navy when he was only twenty. Crandall received a similar challenge in the military when he was twenty-three. Gerstner became the youngest MBA-educated partner in McKinsey's history and had a variety of major challenges before his thirtieth birthday; he was, for example, the lead consultant in the restructuring of the bankrupt Penn Central Corporation. Carlzon was made president of a troubled firm called Vingresor when he was only thirty-two. Nicolosi ran a soft drink business in an extremely competitive marketplace at the age of thirty-four.

Receiving these opportunities is sometimes mostly an accident. Lod Cook, for one, turned a chance event in 1977, a fire at one of the Alaska pipeline's pumping stations, into a terrific experience and a monumental business success; he found a drag–reducing agent called Slickum, obtained a good price for it from a supplier, convinced a reluctant group of pipeline owners to risk adding it to the oil being transported, and thus increased the pipeline's pumping capacity by an incredible 50 percent.

But more often than not, people like Cook received these important challenges because someone was impressed with their potential, and was willing to take a chance on them. ICI's former chairman, Sir John Harvey-Jones, speaks for many individuals like himself when he says: "Looking back I am constantly amazed and grateful for the high risks that others took by giving me responsibility in my early years in ICI. Indeed I have often chided myself with the realization that I have not lived up to the standards that they set."

Harvey-Jones remembers, for example, being called just after he joined the Heavy Organic Chemicals division, and asked by the then–chairman of the division, Tom Clarke, to take charge of a company mission to investigate the price of naphtha. "Naphtha at that time represented half of the firm's total costs, and was bought by central purchasing in London. The division, which prided itself on its knowledge of the oil companies and the oil world, believed that ICI was paying more for naphtha than was necessary.

"At that time, there had been an immense row inside ICI, and it had been agreed that a mission should be sent round the world to investigate the actuality of the situation. I had been in the division only about three months, and barely knew what naphtha was. It had not been my direct responsibility to purchase it and I was operating in a field where everyone else—the companies from which I might buy, those from which we now bought, and the management of the division—was an expert. Nevertheless, with all my lack of experience, the chairman of the division unhesitatingly gave me the responsibility for leading the mission, and it proved to be a turning point in my career. Perhaps because I was unaware of the enormity of the task I had been set, I went at it with tremendous dash and verve, and together with my two colleagues, nominated from other parts of the company, visited no less than twenty companies in eight countries in three weeks. The results formed a report which was out within a month, and which led to far-reaching changes in our company's approach to the problem. I learnt an enormous amount during the process."[2]

Although they sometimes fail when given opportunities like this, most often people like Harvey-Jones succeed. As such, they put together excellent track records which provide credibility that is so essential, especially to the alignment aspects of leadership. Adamson would not have gotten the job at Dundee nor the initial cooperation he received there had it not been for his successful track record at Honeywell and ITT. Likewise, Mayer would never have received support from suppliers and franchisees for the Chicken Littles project if not for his proven record in helping turn KFC around.

People like Dick Mayer also usually have opportunities early in their careers to watch individuals who are good leaders, and thus to learn from direct observation and interaction. This can be particularly important if they are able to watch someone who is skilled at some aspect of leadership where they are weak, e.g., when a cerebral individual who does not know how to motivate others is given an inspirational boss.

Negative role models can be equally important.[3] Sometimes the pain associated with poor leadership makes the lessons particularly powerful. Mary Kay, for example, has said many times over the years that she learned a great deal about leadership from terrible bosses. She remembers once spending ten days on a round-trip bus ride from Texas to Massachusetts with fifty-seven other sales people, making a home-office pilgrimage that was to be their reward for being sales leaders. It was a horrible trip, with several bus breakdowns, but they were willing to endure it, she tells people today, "for the pot of gold at the end of the rainbow: meeting the president of the company as guests in his home. But instead we were given a tour of the plant. Now, a manufacturing plant can be very interesting and a nice place to work—ours is. But I was there to meet the president. When we were finally invited to the president's home, we were only allowed to walk through his rose garden, and we never even had an opportunity to meet with him personally. What a letdown! Needless to say, it was a very long and quiet bus trip back to Texas for all fifty-eight of us."

On another occasion, Mary Kay was attending an all-day sales seminar and was anxious to shake hands with the sales manager, who had delivered an inspiring speech. After waiting in line for three hours it was finally her turn to meet him. "He never even looked at me," she says. "Instead he looked over my shoulder to see how much longer the line was. He wasn't even aware that he was shaking my hand. And although I realized how tired he must have been, I, too, had been there for three hours and was just as tired! I was hurt and offended because he had treated me as if I didn't even exist. Right on the spot I made a decision that if I ever became someone whom people waited in line to shake hands with, I'd give the person in front of me my undivided attention—no matter how tired I was!"[4]

Role models, both good and bad, and challenging experiences, are usually found early in these people's careers. Later, something equally important happens, related to broadening. People who provide effective leadership in big jobs almost always have a chance, before they get into those big jobs, to grow beyond the narrow base that characterizes most managerial careers. This usually is due to lateral career moves or an early promotion to unusually broad job assignments. Sometimes other vehicles help: special task-force assignments or a lengthy general management course. Whatever the case, the breadth of knowledge developed in this way seems to be helpful in all aspects of leadership. So does the network of relationships that is often acquired both inside and outside the firm. When a significant number of people get opportunities like this, the relationships that are built also help create the thick informal networks needed to support multiple leadership initiatives.

Adamson had line and staff roles, manufacturing and engineering jobs, all while he was still relatively young. Gerstner faced a very broad set of consulting assignments while still in his twenties. Cook had direct exposure from his education and early assignments to engineering, labor relations, personnel, marketing, and general management. Crandall had line and staff jobs and served in engineering, planning, and manufacturing. Nicolosi had exposure to engineering, manufacturing, advertising, sales, marketing, and general management, all before his thirty-fifth birthday.

In terms of detail, there is no simple pattern. The exact kinds of broadening experiences these people received varies enormously. The precise nature of the challenges they faced and the timing of these challenges does also. The same can be said about the mentors or bosses from whom they learned things. But again and again, one sees these kinds of career experiences—experiences which equip people with the information, the relationships, the skills, and the track records (sources of power[5]) needed to handle the difficult challenges inherent in big leadership jobs.

A more or less typical example of how these experiences manifest themselves in a single career can be seen in the case of the person who, as much as anyone, is responsible for Pepsi's success over the past few years. His name is Roger Enrico, and as a president of Pepsi, he has helped to double sales and to increase operating profits by 545 percent between 1984 and 1988.[6]

Enrico was born in Chisholm, Minnesota, in 1945, and spent his entire youth there. He performed adequately in school, enjoyed acting, was elected president of his high school class, and did some work in a local soft drink bottling plant. At Babson College in Wellesley, Massachusetts, he performed well academically, ran his fraternity and the student court, edited the yearbook, and graduated in three years. He joined Minneapolis-based General Mills in its personnel function for a short time after college and when the Vietnam War intruded, he enlisted in the Navy Officer Candidate program.

The Navy sent him to Supply Officer School for six months and then to Southeast Asia. In Vietnam he found his first post-education mentor, Lt. Commander Bill Alenderter, and his first set of major on-the-job challenges. Alenderter and his troops were in charge of fuel operations for I-Corps, located in the northern-most part of South Vietnam. Their job was to find several million gallons of fuel each week from tens of different and unreliable sources, and then to ship the fuel to hundreds of different and always changing places, despite the Vietcong and typhoons.

Alenderter taught Enrico to take calculated risks when necessary to get the job done, and gave him the opportunity to do just that. Usually he succeeded, sometimes he failed, but in either case he learned: the importance of being bold and innovative in your thinking when working under difficult circumstances, the critical need to listen carefully to what experienced people have to say, and the danger in believing in your own infallibility.

From Vietnam he went to the Sixth Fleet in the Mediterranean and then back to General Mills, this time in brand management. As an assistant brand manager for products like Betty Crocker pancake mix, and then, after a promotion, Wheaties, Enrico learned something about living with responsibility without much formal authority, and the need to proactively champion your cause in that environment. He found another mentor, Steve Chase, his marketing director. But he also bumped up against a somewhat sluggish bureaucracy, and one senior person in that bureaucracy who turned him off. Young and impatient, Enrico decided to leave and take a job at Frito-Lay, a division of PepsiCo.

Starting at Frito-Lay in Dallas as an associate brand manager in a small but well-run marketing department, he performed exceptionally well. Three promotions came in rapid succession, making him a very young marketing director responsible for several hundreds of millions of dollars worth of business. During this time he learned a great deal about the business itself from Jim O'Neal, the senior vice-president for operations, and about motivating people from Jimmy Sappington, the man who built Frito's route-sales system.

In 1975, after two years of exposure to the company's unsuccessful business in Japan, Enrico stuck his neck out and recommended that PepsiCo make a major change of course there; instead of continuing to try to build a U.S.-like distribution system, he argued that it should use the Japanese wholesale distribution system and team up with a local firm in a joint venture. One thing led to another, and Enrico was offered the presidency of PepsiCo Foods Japan. Now conventional wisdom at Frito-Lay and most companies is that an international assignment, far from the home office, is very risky. Such a job takes one away from the real action, from one's mentors, and from the fast track. But Enrico had already learned that risk-averse conventional wisdom is not the best guide in life. So he took the job.

Life in Japan, thousands of miles away from bosses and peers in the United States, in a completely new culture, and with a poorly performing business, was tough. After much work, he did set up a joint venture, Fujiya-Frito-Lay, and in the process learned a great deal. While it was still struggling to become a success, Enrico was given a major promotion and shipped to Brazil, to be a Pepsi-Cola International area vice-president. Brazil turned out to be even tougher. As little as he knew about the snack food business in Japan, he knew even less about the soft drink business in Brazil. And there he encountered a boss with whom he had great difficulty.

During his fifteen months in South America, Enrico floundered. He became much more involved in company politics than ever before, or after, and he had great difficulty getting things done. He did learn about the business, but his biggest lessons were from his boss—what not to do—and from his own behavior; you can fail, he found out, if you get into a tough situation and then try to survive by being cautious and political.

His mentors at PepsiCo, especially Andy Pearson, brought him back to the States and made him vice-president of marketing for Frito-Lay. In light of his past accomplishments, this was an easier job, and Enrico performed exceptionally well. Two years later, in 1980, he was made senior vice-president of sales and marketing for the Pepsi-Cola Bottling Group—the bottling operation owned by Pepsi. He did well there too, and learned more from people like Pearson and PepsiCo CEO Don Kendall. In 1982, Pepsi President John Sculley asked him to be the executive vice-president and chief operating officer of Pepsi-Cola USA—the franchise group of bottling operations. In this job, he became more and more involved with the big money, TV-focused, advertising business. In 1983, when John Sculley went to Apple Computer, Enrico took over his job.

Only a few months after becoming president of Pepsi, Enrico signed the most expensive celebrity advertising contract ever: $5 million, for two commercials and for allowing Pepsi to sponsor a concert tour. More than a few people thought this move was foolish—the risk, much too big. Some had not even heard of the celebrity, or had heard disturbing things about him. Enrico moved ahead anyway, trusting judgment that was the product of an interesting set of experiences.

It paid off. The Michael Jackson commercials were among the most successful in the entire history of the soft drink industry.

Enrico's career is far from the norm. For the vast majority of people today, including most of those with leadership potential, on-the-job experiences actually seem to undermine the development of attributes needed for leadership. Evidence from studies I have conducted strongly suggests that managerial careers in many corporations produce individuals who are remarkably narrow in focus and understanding, moderately risk averse, weak in communication skills, and relatively blind to the values of others. They produce people who know little about competitive business strategies, who have limited credibility, and who know more about how to play games with a budget than how to celebrate the real achievements of their people. They create individuals who are moderately competent at management (not highly competent), and not at all competent at leadership.[7]

Four characteristics of managerial careers seem to be particularly important in producing these results. First, these careers usually begin in centralized and specialized hierarchies and, as such, in jobs that are narrow in scope and tactical in focus. In large firms in particular, people spend years and years in these kinds of jobs, even if they are promoted many times. As a result, individuals learn to deal with short-term issues, but not the long term; tactics, but not strategy; and specialized functional problems, not general business issues.

Related to this, promotions in many firms are almost entirely up a narrow, vertical hierarchy. The junior accountant becomes an accountant, then a senior accountant, and then perhaps an assistant controller. As a result, the knowledge and relationship base of successful people is often extremely narrow; they understand only one aspect of the business and only one group of people in their corporations. Furthermore, their credibility tends to be extremely limited too; people like themselves may know and respect them, but most others will not.

Especially talented and ambitious individuals often move up these narrow hierarchies at great speed. Ten promotions in ten to fifteen years are not unusual. Moving through jobs every twelve to eighteen months, these people rarely have an opportunity to learn anything in-depth, and never see the longer-term consequences of their actions. This career pattern often produces a short-term focus, a manipulative management style, and a track record of accomplishments that can be viewed with considerable suspicion.

A fourth characteristic of managerial careers in many organizations is perhaps the most damaging of all. All too often, people are rewarded almost exclusively for short-term results. As a consequence, most individuals focus on the process that produces those results—management. This is especially true for ambitious young people. Because of this, they learn some important lessons about management, but they learn little about leadership. Since developing the leadership potential of others is also not a short-term activity, senior executives are strongly encouraged by such reward systems not to invest time in such an activity. The overall result can be devastating.

In total, these common career patterns develop talented people into managers, although not exceptional ones, over a period of ten to twenty years. Those who are most successful end up in jobs at age forty or fifty that demand a considerable amount of leadership, and those positions usually stretch them in that direction. But there are limits to how fast even the most talented of people can develop, and at age fifty or sixty some find themselves in a very different place, vis-à-vis the capacity to provide strong leadership, than people like Dick Mayer or Lod Cook (see Exhibit 9.1).

These patterns are so prevalent in so many organizations today that people sometimes view them as inevitable. But they are not.

The career experiences of Enrico, Adamson, Gerstner, and Carlzon, although relatively rare today, are much more commonly found in some firms than others. Enrico, for example, is only one of many people at PepsiCo who have had high-quality on-the-job experiences. In such corporations, these experiences tend to be directly related to certain practices that, in a sense, systematically create more of those careers than one finds in most organizations.[8] In this way, these firms empower significant numbers of people to handle potentially difficult leadership challenges.

For example, corporations that do a much better-than-average job of developing leadership potential put an emphasis on creating chal-

Exhibit 9.1 *The Growth of Leadership and Management Capacity Over the Span of a Career*

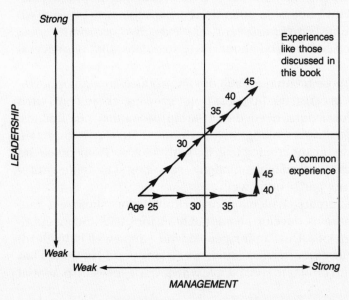

lenging opportunities for relatively young employees. They do so in a number of ways. In many firms, decentralization is the key. By definition, decentralization pushes responsibility lower in an organization and in the process creates more challenging jobs at lower levels. Johnson & Johnson, 3M, Hewlett-Packard, General Electric, and a number of other well-known firms have used that approach quite successfully in the past. Some of those same firms also create as many small units as possible so there are lots of challenging, lower-level, general management jobs available. GE, HP, and J&J are said to have benefited greatly over the years from that approach.

Sometimes these firms develop additional challenging opportunities by stressing growth through new products or services. Over the years, 3M has had a policy that at least 25 percent of its revenue should come from products introduced within the last five years. That encourages small new ventures, which in turn offer hundreds of opportunities to test and stretch young people with leadership potential. Some of these same firms also work hard to minimize bureaucracy and rigid structures so that it is easier to enhance jobs with additional challenges. As an executive at Coca-Cola put it: "If I hire an MBA as a brand manager, because we are not highly compartmentalized and structured, he or she can make that job into almost anything. The person is not in a box. We can make the job as big and challenging as is necessary to really turn that person on."

Other firms, including some that face limits to how much they can decentralize responsibility into small units, create specific jobs to challenge people with leadership potential. Perhaps the most obvious example is administrative assistant (or executive assistant) jobs. Anheuser-Busch has created about thirty such jobs. IBM has several hundred.

When all of those techniques still do not produce enough opportunities, perhaps because the business is not growing, these firms then take the painful actions needed to free up promotion possibilities. That sometimes means making early retirement attractive to certain people. It always means coming to grips with "blockers"—people who have no chance of further promotion, are a long way from retirement, and are not performing well.

Practices that create challenging opportunities for employees can, almost by themselves, develop people qualified for small- and medium-sized leadership jobs. Developing people who can do well in big leadership jobs requires more work, often over a long period of time. That work begins with efforts to spot people with great leadership potential early in their careers and to identify just what will be needed to stretch and develop that potential.

The methods these firms use are surprisingly straightforward. They go out of their way to make young employees and people at lower levels in their organizations visible to senior management. Senior managers then judge for themselves who has potential and what the development needs of those people are. Executives then discuss their tentative conclusions openly and candidly, among themselves, in an effort to draw more and more accurate judgments. "Scientific" techniques seem to be rarely employed. The key is: look, talk, and think.

To make younger employees visible to senior management, a variety of methods are used. Johnson & Johnson regularly takes young people who someone thinks has potential and puts them on special projects that conclude with presentations to senior management. "I can still remember making a presentation when I was thirty years old to a group that included the chairman of the company," says one executive at J&J. "Once a month, I have a luncheon with one of my key functional managers, and I always ask that he or she bring some high-potential employees along. At certain staff meetings, I do the same thing. This allows me to get to know a lot of young people and to draw my own conclusions about potential, strengths, and weaknesses" says a senior official at Coca-Cola. An executive at Dow Jones says, "We don't let the organizational structure constrain us. We always go right to the individual who has information we need. This puts us in contact with a lot of lower-level and more junior employees, and gives us a firsthand feeling for who they are and what they are good at."

At General Mills there are many recognition programs that often bring good people to the attention of senior management. These make good people more visible, which is very helpful. At Hewlett-Packard, says one executive, "One of the things we do is to set up situations which allow our divisions to put their best people 'on stage.' And then we take a hard look. In this way, you can spot promising young people, and once you know their names, you can go out of your way to get to know them better." At Anheuser-Busch the top people make it a habit to get out to the plants on a regular basis. This gives them a chance to meet and to talk to younger employees, and makes them visible to senior executives who would never meet them otherwise.

These kinds of practices provide senior managers with information on people who might have leadership potential. Executives then

share and discuss that information among themselves, either informally or formally, on a regular basis. The Management Council at
Hewlett-Packard, for example, has had regular discussions about the
middle management at the company, and the discussions are reported to be very open. Large firms tend to try to do that sort of thing
in a very systematic way. At Du Pont, the sixteen senior department
heads meet once a month for two hours. At a typical meeting, the
agenda includes a discussion of the half-dozen people one of those
executives thinks are highly promotable. Before these meetings, pictures and biographies of those six people are sent to all department
heads. At the meeting, everyone who knows those people is expected
to speak up, especially those who have concerns or questions about a
person's potential (e.g., "When Harry worked for us five years ago, he
only performed at an average level. What has happened to him recently that led you to think so highly of him?"). People who do not
know the candidate being discussed are also expected to be aggressive in their questioning (e.g., "How does she compare to George
Smith?" "How well did he do in his one staff assignment?"). Such a
process can work very well, although there are many pitfalls that
must be avoided: allowing irrelevant personal preferences/biases to
affect the discussion (i.e., "women can't lead"), picking people based
on today's or yesterday's needs instead of tomorrow's, or putting labels on people (e.g., a winner, a loser) that become unfair, self-
fulfilling prophecies.

Armed with a better-than-average sense of who has considerable
leadership potential and what needs to be developed in those people,
executives in these firms then spend time planning for that development. Sometimes that is done as a part of a formal succession planning or high-potential development process. Often it is done more
informally. In either case, the key ingredient appears to be an intelligent assessment of what feasible development opportunities fit each
candidate's needs; unlike some firms, these companies do not have
generic formulas for developing all their high-potential people (e.g.,
one year in marketing and then one year in finance, etc.).

Developmental opportunities, in the sense that term is being used
here, include:

- New job assignments (promotions and lateral moves)
- Formal training (inside the firm, at a public seminar, or at a
  university)
- Task force or committee assignments

- Mentoring or coaching from a senior executive
- Attendance at meetings outside a person's core responsibility
- Special projects
- Special development jobs (e.g., executive assistant jobs)

To encourage managers to participate in all of these activities, such firms tend to recognize developmental successes and reward managers for them. This is rarely done as a part of a formal compensation or bonus formula, simply because it is so difficult to measure developmental successes with precision. But it does become a factor in promotion decisions, especially to the most senior levels. And that seems to make a big difference.

When told that future promotions will depend to some degree on their ability to develop leaders, even people who say that leadership cannot be developed often somehow find ways to do just that; usually they try to reduce career experiences that do not nurture leadership potential and increase those that do (see Exhibit 9.2).

Some people have the capacity to become excellent managers but not very strong leaders. Others have great leadership potential but, for a variety of reasons, have great difficulty becoming strong managers. Smart companies value both kinds of individuals and work hard to make them a part of the overall team. But when it comes to grooming people for executive jobs, such firms ignore the recent literature that says people cannot manage and lead, and focus their efforts on individuals that seem to have the potential to do both. That is, they try to develop more leader-managers than managers and leaders, and for one very important reason.

Leadership and management are sufficiently different that they can easily conflict. A firm made up mostly of leaders and managers often polarizes into two warring camps, eventually resulting in one side winning (usually the managerial camp because it is bigger) and then in the purging of the other side. In firms with a large contingent of leader-managers, this rarely happens.

Developing enough leader-managers to help run the huge number of complex organizations that dominate our society today is a great challenge. But it is a challenge we must accept. The more pessimistic among us think this is hopeless. Some even argue that there is no such thing as a leader-manager. They are clearly wrong; most of the individuals discussed in the book both lead and manage. At this point, it is

Exhibit 9.2 *Career Experiences and Leadership*

	Career Experiences	Effect on Leadership
Promotes leadership	Challenging assignments early in a career	Stretches people, helping them to grow in many dimensions, some of which will be relevant to leadership; allows individuals to try leadership and learn from their successes and failures
	Visible leadership role models who are very good or very bad	Extreme examples, both good and bad, are easy to learn from, because the lessons are very clear
	Assignments which broaden	Breadth of knowledge is particularly important for direction setting, and breadth of contacts and relationships for alignment and motivation
Inhibits leadership	A long series of narrow and tactical jobs	Makes one short-term and tactically oriented; does not develop long-term and strategic skills
	Vertical career movement	Does not produce the breadth needed to lead in big jobs
	Rapid promotions	Does not help people to think long term or to learn the impact of their actions over the long term; can encourage a manipulative style
	Measurement and rewards based on short-term results only	Encourages people to pay attention to the management aspects of their jobs and ignore the leadership aspects; teaches management but not leadership

thing as a leader-manager. They are clearly wrong; most of the individuals discussed in the book both lead and manage. At this point, it is simply not clear how many more of these people would emerge if the circumstances were right. The only way to find out—is to try.

10

Corporate Culture

A ll corporations that have some minimum continuity of personnel and purpose eventually develop cultures, both for the organization as a whole and for different subunits. These cultures can become very strong, like those at Dow, Shell, or IBM,[1] where many people share certain values and believe in similar approaches to conducting business which express those values. Both strong and weak cultures can influence the amount of effective leadership in an organization. Sometimes they affect it most powerfully.

Culture is important for our purposes here in at least three different ways. It can influence whether executives look for and develop people with leadership potential, or whether they do not. It can influence whether people with leadership ability are encouraged to lead, or whether they are discouraged. It can even help determine whether a firm has the kind of informal networks needed to make multiple leadership initiatives converge (see Exhibit 10.1).

For example, in a study of practices in fifteen firms with reputations for doing a superior job of attracting and developing people with leadership potential, culture was identified as the critical force supporting those practices. Again and again that factor emerged in interviews with senior executives.[2] An executive at 3M talked about it this way: "First of all, we feel that we have an obligation to broaden and stretch people. That's just the way we are. People that don't think that way—people low in integrity that are just out for themselves, for example—don't do well around here. We try to take risks with people to stretch them. We don't mind giving people a little rope, even early

127

Exhibit 10.1 *Corporate Culture and Leadership*

Corporate Culture

Norms and shared values relevant to leadership:

- The kind of people that are valued in middle and senior management (leaders or not, leadership potential or not) and the normal practices for hiring and developing them

- The kind of behavior valued from people (leadership or not) and the practices that encourage that behavior

- The number and strength of shared values which bind people together in informal networks, and the practices which acculturate new employees to those values

---

Leadership

The amount of leadership in the corporation and how well it converges (or conflicts)

---

in their careers here. The culture supports risk taking. And if it doesn't work out, we don't shoot people. The environment here is also pretty open and family-like. As such, it's relatively easy to move people across departments or divisions for development purposes. And young people feel comfortable, in this environment, to go talk to senior people outside their immediate groups about possible future job opportunities. We know our culture has helped us to prosper in the past and we are trying to consciously maintain and renew it."

An executive at Citicorp had this to say: "Managers around here wouldn't think of trying to hire second-class people. Trying to find the best is too deeply embedded in the fabric of the place. Senior executives ask questions. If a unit doesn't hire good people, they will find that out. Also, after you have been here a while, you learn that in order to succeed, you have got to hire and develop good people. I can think of a couple of very talented managers who haven't done well here. Part of their problem was that they didn't create a strong staff underneath them. They didn't go out and get good people and then broaden them, which is the way you do things around here." A manager at Morgan Guaranty talked about the same sort of thing this way: "Our team-oriented culture simply doesn't allow people to play political games like hiding their good, young employees. People gang up against someone like that. It also makes lateral transfers for development relatively easy to produce. We value broad-based people and have a tradition of sorts of producing them."

Beyond its impact on the recruitment and development of people with leadership potential, culture also influences whether employees will actually try to provide leadership. Some corporate cultures value risk taking, communication, celebrations, and adaptive change. Some do not. In either case, it can make a huge difference.

Many of the initial activities of Gerstner and Nicolosi were aimed at creating cultures that would encourage leadership. They recognized that their actions alone would be far from sufficient, that winning intensely competitive battles would require competent leadership at every level in their organizations. They also knew that their firms had some people with leadership capacity, perhaps many. The challenge was to create an environment which would encourage them to use those abilities.

Nicolosi and Gerstner also understood that leadership can conflict, that without a lot of shared values and teamwork, the various leadership initiatives might not converge. As a result, they tried to develop cultures that not only valued leadership, but that also encouraged shared visions and good working relationships among bosses, subordinates, and peers. To a large degree, they succeeded.

Dallas Kirk and his team at Digital didn't have to construct a new culture; a useful one already existed. People who know the firm, describe it with words like informal, network-like, can-do oriented, entrepreneurial, non-dictatorial, and honest. That culture was enormously important in helping to encourage leadership for Decworld and to keep those initiatives moving in compatible directions. It is very hard to even imagine an event like that being successful, no matter how talented the individuals involved, without this kind of a culture.

The power of certain types of cultures to help produce effective leadership is most certainly great. Situations like the ones at TRS (American Express) or Decworld are a testament to this conclusion. But even those cases do not make this point as dramatically as the story of the Omaha-based food giant called ConAgra.[3]

ConAgra's roots are in flour milling, and date back to 1867. In that post-Civil War year, Henry Koenig and Frederick Wiebe built a steam-powered grain mill in Grand Island, Nebraska. Henry Glade bought that mill in 1883 and built, over the next twenty-seven years, a small milling business. After his death, his firm and three similar businesses were incorporated in 1919 as the Nebraska Consolidated Mills Company, the name by which ConAgra was known until 1971.

NCMC grew internally and through acquisitions in the 1920s and 1930s. In 1941, using a by-product of milling, it branched into feed-grain production. In 1956 it added a third business, poultry, to use some of its feed-grain output. All three of NCMC's product lines grew in the 1960s, and in 1970, an acquisition added catfish. To reflect this diversification beyond just milling, in 1971 the firm's name was changed to ConAgra. Revenues in 1972, some 105 years after the opening of the first flour mill, reached $302 million.

The years 1973 and 1974 brought difficult times. The economic miracle following World War II was dying, if not dead. Inflation was rising rapidly. Volatility in many markets was increasing. As a result, ConAgra's interest payments on money borrowed to make acquisitions rose rapidly. Some of these acquisitions performed poorly in a sluggish economy. Price controls in Puerto Rico hurt one of its most profitable operations. In a more uncertain commodities market, the firm made a few disastrous transactions. The net result was a loss of $11.8 million in 1974, and a market valuation that sank to $10 million.

To turn this around, in August 1974, the board of directors named Claude Carter, a thirty-three-year veteran with the firm, as president. Carter's first major act was to hire a COO from outside the firm—one Mike Harper. On October 1, 1974, he joined ConAgra as executive vice-president.

Harper grew up in Lansing, Michigan, and South Bend, Indiana. He graduated from Purdue in 1949 with a mechanical engineering degree. After receiving an MBA from the University of Chicago, he went to work for General Motors. Five years later he moved to Pillsbury. Starting there as an industrial engineer, he went on to become director of engineering, vice-president of R & D, head of the Food Service Supply Division, and then group vice-president of Fresh Poultry and Food Service Supply.

Upon arrival at ConAgra, Harper found a strong commitment to being the low-cost producer, a commitment that was shared by most of the management. He also found a good work ethic. On the negative side, he encountered a firm that had been highly centralized, had few performance measures that would allow anyone to really delegate, was very hierarchical and formal, was weak at marketing and selling, and did not seem to care enough about profit.

Almost immediately, Harper put a large corkboard on one of his office walls and filled it with charts showing how all his businesses were doing on sales, income, inventories, and a few other measures. He then began calling each general manager every Monday morning to update those charts. At first, many of those managers could not tell him what their inventory levels were, or how much money they made the previous week, because they had not been traditionally asked to be responsible for those results. That changed.

During his first year at ConAgra, Harper looked for and found many opportunities to bring those managers together to talk about the business. His whole approach communicated that he saw them as businessmen, not factory managers, and an important part of the executive team. He introduced them to the idea that they were responsible for managing both their income statements and their balance sheets. He showed them how inventories and receivables were hurting ConAgra's bottom line and pushed them to reduce both.

The sale of a few unpromising and poorly performing assets, in combination with reduced inventories and receivables, raised badly needed cash, paid off nearly half the outstanding debt, and put the firm back in the black. The turnaround came quickly; for fiscal 1975 ConAgra made $4.1 million. In March 1976, Harper was appointed CEO.

As soon as the firm was making money again, Harper pressed ahead with longer-term questions: What kind of a business should this be? And how should we manage ourselves? His experiences at Pillsbury had left him with numerous ideas about how a food business should be managed. Some of these came directly from former CEO's like Bob Keith and Terry Hanold. Other ideas came from negative experiences—things that he saw that he did not like.

In October, Harper brought a group of seven people to Vail, Colorado, to address these issues. They talked informally, candidly, and intensely for two-and-a-half days, and in the process came to a general agreement on a number of points. ConAgra, they felt, should be a basic food company with products and services across the entire food chain. (This later evolved into "a *global* basic food company.") The firm should strive to produce a return on equity of at least 15 percent each year, and an average ROE over a period of years of 20 percent. It should also set a growth goal of doubling its size.

After returning to Omaha, Harper began writing a "white paper" in which he included the ideas developed at that meeting plus additional thoughts of his own. He circulated a draft to all of his top executives and operating officers and urged them to comment. They did. The document was discussed and rewritten a number of different times. When his top group was satisfied, they shared a draft with their middle-level managers and urged them to provide feedback. After still more rewriting, the paper was published in July 1977 as a small booklet. This published version of the white paper was given to all ConAgra employees. Later, it was also provided to security analysts, potential employees, and acquisition candidates.

The booklet was entitled "ConAgra's Philosophy." Written statements of goals, values, visions, and the like often seem to have little relationship to how firms actually operate. But the ideas in this remarkable little booklet accurately reflect the corporate culture that has emerged at ConAgra.

"ConAgra's Philosophy" starts with a letter from Mike Harper. (An updated version of the booklet published in 1984 has a letter from the top eight executives.) Harper begins by saying: "The perspectives that you will find in the booklet were developed to guide us all in building a better ConAgra. The turnaround achieved by ConAgra in 1975, after an almost disastrous year in fiscal 1974, was accomplished by people, [a] combination of key, long–service ConAgrans and experienced people new to the company. ConAgra has emerged as a 'new' company, soundly financed, with a higher level of earning power, and with a new operating philosophy. With the turnaround accomplished, we were able to then devote our attention during fiscal 1976 to the future of the company.

"Our objective is to increase the earning power of the company over an extended period of time in order to increase the return to our stockholders, and to increase the security of our employees. High rates of return on invested capital, coupled with growing earnings, generate the cash and financing power needed to support the future growth of the company. Obviously, earnings growth must be consistent with our public and social responsibilities, but in the end our fundamental objective must be an unabashed pursuit of profit [through] the delivery of quality products and services to customers.

"From our planning process, we have identified certain businesses and assets which will be the base for a much larger and stronger ConAgra. Risk decisions have been made; strategic plans have been laid; and the task of building earnings has begun. More opportunities for growth in size and profitability are being sought and will be identified and pursued in the future. Earnings growth will come from a combination of innovative marketing, aggressive selling, business de-velopment and planning, a low-cost production posture versus our competition, in addition to good financial controls. The critical re-sources involved in building a great company are made up of individ-uals and the way in which they manage. The following pages contain our overall objectives, a guiding business philosophy, the climate and organizational structure in which we operate, and a definition of the quality of people that we need."

In a relatively short section on "Objectives," the pamphlet lists a number of quantifiable financial goals: an average return for stock-holder equity in excess of 15 percent (the 1984 booklet raises this to 20 percent), an average growth in trend-line earnings of 10 percent per year (raised in 1984 to 14 percent), and the maintenance of a relatively conservative balance sheet. A much longer section on "Busi-ness Philosophy" begins with a most revealing sentence: "The Corner-stone: The company's success will depend on entrepreneurial leadership coupled with professional management operating in an atmosphere of openness that encourages top-quality, innovative, profit-minded people to achieve results." Following this is a discussion of "Our Current Business," "Growth of the Present Business," "Growth Beyond our Existing Business," and "The Conduct of Our Affairs."

In a section on "Organizational Climate," Harper says that creating the proper environment is probably the most important task that management can undertake. "Our objectives are to create a culture that: facilitates and emphasizes striving for high goals and high stan-dards, emphasizes developing people and ideas, emphasizes high par-ticipation and high involvement between managers and their people, and emphasizes collaboration and close professional association among peers—where rivalries between departments are de-emphasized and instead we focus on the objectives that unify us rather than those that are divisive." This section includes discussion on the conditions needed to create this culture, and stresses: freedom to act, responsibility for end results, freedom to disagree and chal-lenge, development of people, building competence, and recognizing individuality. Under this last topic, the booklet points out: "Some of the basic beliefs we have are: 1) Most people want to be involved meaningfully in their work. 2) Most people want to feel connected to and a part of a larger world (a sense of belonging). 3) Most people want to set goals and use their energies to attain them. And 4) Most people would like to be their own person, and to feel a sense of responsibility, as well as a sense of personal uniqueness, and the freedom to express themselves as they are."

The booklet goes on to talk about quality of people. Among other things, it says "We will place a significant value on the individual manager's performance in leadership and the ability to attract, retain, and develop top-quality people at all levels in his or her organization. We must commit ourselves to doing a better job than our competitors in developing the people in ConAgra." Finally, the booklet describes the organization of the company, the management executive committee and management council, the strategic and annual plan, the quarterly reviews and the Monday morning meetings. It concludes by saying that: "ConAgra's organizational structure is one that has a minimum of levels, one that must operate with a great deal of decentralization, with adequate controls, and one that has a great deal of flexibility."

In 1977 and 1978, Harper and his top team began trying to make this philosophy a reality. For a number of reasons, they were largely successful. The key was probably Harper, whose actions were virtually always consistent with the major points in the pamphlet. This large (six foot five), warm, bear of a man both led and managed with great effectiveness. Over time, this helped drive a set of values into the organization and create a strong culture; in a 1988 survey of food executives, ConAgra was seen as having the strongest culture among the eleven largest firms in its industry.[4] It even created a ConAgra culture in acquisitions that were accustomed to doing business in a very different way. The case of Banquet is a good example.

Banquet Frozen Foods has roots that go back to 1898 when a Missourian school teacher named Finis Stamper began to supplement his income by marketing poultry and eggs. In 1903, he built a poultry processing plant in Clifton Hills, Missouri, and in 1913 added a creamery. A decade later, the F.M. Stamper Company started processing frozen egg whites for bakeries; the frozen yolks were sold to mayonnaise producers. In 1928, the firm added a line of feeds for hogs, poultry, and cattle. During World War II, it produced canned chicken products for American soldiers. After the War, the company began selling frozen chicken pies in newly developed and inexpensive aluminum packages. Soon came other frozen products sold under the Banquet name: meat pies, dinners, fruit pies, and fried chicken. The frozen foods turned out to be very popular.

In 1970, RCA bought the Stamper Company for $116.5 million and

changed its name to Banquet. After a disastrous ten years, RCA sold
most of that firm to ConAgra for $55 million.

RCA is the electronics firm built largely by David Sarnoff. When he
died in 1966, the company undertook an acquisitions binge that
brought in Hertz (car rental), Random House (publishing), Cushman
& Wakefield (real estate), and Coronet (furniture and carpets), as well
as Banquet. Conglomerization, however, did not work, and RCA's
earnings declined greatly. During this period, there was continuous
turnover at the top, along with considerable bureaucracy and politics
at the Rockefeller Center headquarters. Management's focus shrunk
to the short term and only financial results were discussed with divisions like Banquet. Little else could be discussed; few people at Rockefeller Center had experience in the food business.

Under RCA, Banquet developed a variety of unhealthy habits. Work
usually started at 9:00 A.M. and ended at 4:30 P.M. Company cars pro-
liferated. Any entrepreneurial spirit died; the firm introduced no
new products in the 1970s. And despite a booming frozen food market, Banquet's sales and earnings started to decline.

When ConAgra bought Banquet, according to longtime Banquet executives, "You could see the difference immediately." Within a week
of the purchase, Harper called a two-day meeting of those managers
and talked to them about ConAgra's philosophy. They could not believe it: "After ten years of writing memos to faceless staff people in
New York and having quarterly reviews in which we talked about
nothing but short-term numbers, to sit and talk about philosophy,
about his long-term vision, and about strategies in the food business—
well it was a shock, but it was a wonderful shock."

Within a few months Harper looked for and found the person he
felt was the number one frozen food executive in the United States.
His name was John Phillips and he had been working for Campbell in
its Swanson division. Harper asked him to run Banquet. Intrigued by
Harper's style and ConAgra's culture, Phillips accepted, and began
work on January 6, 1981.

After graduating from Utah State University in 1958 with an economics degree, Phillips spent his entire career up to 1981 with Campbell. He started in a canned food plant in Sacramento, where he
worked in purchasing, industrial engineering, product supervision,
and accounting. In 1964, he helped start up a new plant in Texas, and
eventually worked as the assistant superintendent of manufacturing.
He went from there to the Swanson division's poultry operations, and
then to corporate marketing as an advertising manager. He next man-

aged four frozen food plants in Nebraska, ran the Pepperidge Farm subsidiary, served as the corporate director of personnel, and eventually became president of Swanson.

At Banquet, Phillips and his team rebuilt the marketing department, reorganized the sales force, upgraded the quality of a few products, and altered production methods that created unwanted inventory. They built up a market research data base, changed the advertising, and increased the ad budget dramatically. After ten years in which no new products had been introduced, they also began, cautiously at first, trying out new flavors, then new products.

Their first completely new product line was called "Saucy Chicken," five or six pieces of chicken covered with either barbecue sauce, garlic, or butter. The product bombed. Undeterred, they tried other ideas, and soon had a few successes.

Within a very short time, Banquet was once again performing well. After only three years, earnings paid for the purchase price and the new culture introduced by ConAgra took hold. Stronger management and leadership (central tenets of the culture) began to emerge at multiple levels.

In 1982, Harper created an Office of the President at corporate headquarters in Omaha and promoted Phillips into it. He then hired Phil Fletcher, a veteran of Campbell, Heinz, and Heublein, to take Phillips' place. Fletcher's first reaction after coming to Banquet and ConAgra was: "I have never found a business environment like this anywhere I've been. Mike Harper has created a unique culture."

Fletcher and his management team flourished. They focused on improving the division's marketing and sales. Under Fletcher's leadership, and that of his successor, Scott Rahn, Banquet poured out more new products and started to grow fast. Major acquisitions were added in 1984 and 1986. By 1988, the division recorded $1 billion in revenues, a 300 percent increase since 1980.

Visitors to Banquet headquarters in St. Louis in the fall of that year found a sense of excitement among the management there. A very visible plaque in the offices of many of those managers had engraved on it: "Effective Leadership: a leader has a vision and conviction that a dream can be achieved, and inspires the power and energy to get it done."

By 1988, Banquet was one of fifty "independent operating companies" inside ConAgra, each of which was headed by a "president" who was expected to lead, manage, and encourage others to do likewise. The corporation that year recorded overall revenues of $10 billion.

Its income had grown well over 1,000 percent since the first "philosophy" booklet was published. So had its market value. The once-small company based in Omaha, Nebraska, had become the eighth largest food corporation in the world.[5]

There are people, and not a small number of them, who sense the importance of leadership, recognize its scarcity today, and yet do not believe its significant expansion is realistically possible. For these people, direction setting, alignment, and motivation will always be the province of a chosen few. Situations like the one at ConAgra defy this pessimistic view. Such cases show that leadership *can* expand far beyond the norm today. They demonstrate that with careful selection, the nurturing of talent, and encouragement, dozens and dozens of people can play important leadership roles in a single organization. The key is culture.

The right kind of culture can foster both leadership and management, despite differences in function, process, and structure that create a potential for conflict. It can help hundreds of people to create the short-term results expected by an organization's constituencies and the long-term changes needed to adapt to a shifting environment.

Developing a culture that creates strong leadership and management is probably difficult under any circumstances. In large, older organizations, creating the right vision and values, if they do not already exist, can be an awesome task. Institutionalizing such a culture, so that it does not disintegrate after the creator has left, is even tougher.[6] Doing this demands great skill, perseverance, and not a small amount of courage. But for those who are successful, the payoff is gigantic: in terms of long-term economic results, the quality of life offered to employees over the length of their careers, the overall package of goods and services offered to customers over a decade or more, and the general benefits to society.

Nowhere is this clearer than in a time of crisis, the ultimate example of an unstable and changing environment demanding competent leadership. Many corporations today look inept, if not just plain evil, when a major crisis erupts. Lacking a broad vision of their responsibilities, the alignment of their employees to such a vision, or the capacity to motivate people to execute all that, these firms freeze under the pressure of a crisis or take actions that ultimately hurt both themselves and others. Organizations that are well led stand out under these circumstances; consider Johnson & Johnson, a firm well known for better-than-average leadership in its management hierarchy, and its response to the Tylenol tragedy.

Developing a culture that creates strong leadership and management requires doing the sorts of things Harper and his executive team appear to have done (to some degree, the same can be said of Adamson, Gerstner, Carlzon, Nicolosi, etc.). This means, first and foremost, providing a vision of the kind of culture that is needed. It also means being a visible role model of what is expected from others. It means helping people to understand what leadership is, why it is important, how it is different from management, and how it can be created. It means giving people the opportunity to lead and manage. It means supporting efforts with resources and enthusiasm that are consistent with the desired culture. It means recognizing and rewarding successes. In short, it means providing leadership on the issue of culture.[7]

Leadership and culture are subjects that are as closely related as management and structure (or systems). It takes strong leadership to create a useful culture. And only with certain kinds of cultures does one find competent leadership emerging throughout an organization.

Just as we clearly need more people who can, collectively, provide leadership to the complex organizations that dominate our world today, we desperately need more people to develop the cultures that will create that leadership. In a sense, institutionalizing a leadership-centered culture is the ultimate act of leadership.

Postscript

The exhibits in this section summarize the major ideas presented in this book.

Comparing Management and Leadership

	Management	Leadership
Creating an agenda	Planning and Budgeting—establishing detailed steps and timetables for achieving needed results, and then allocating the resources necessary to make that happen	Establishing Direction—developing a vision of the future, often the distant future, and strategies for producing the changes needed to achieve that vision
Developing a human network for achieving the agenda	Organizing and Staffing—establishing some structure for accomplishing plan requirements, staffing that structure with individuals, delegating responsibility and authority for carrying out the plan, providing policies and procedures to help guide people, and creating methods or systems to monitor implementation	Aligning People—communicating the direction by words and deeds to all those whose cooperation may be needed so as to influence the creation of teams and coalitions that understand the vision and strategies, and accept their validity
Execution	Controlling and Problem Solving—monitoring results vs. plan in some detail, identifying deviations, and then planning and organizing to solve these problems	Motivating and Inspiring—energizing people to overcome major political, bureaucratic, and resource barriers to change by satisfying very basic, but often unfulfilled, human needs
Outcomes	Produces a degree of predictability and order, and has the potential of consistently producing key results expected by various stakeholders (e.g., for customers, always being on time; for stockholders, being on budget)	Produces change, often to a dramatic degree, and has the potential of producing extremely useful change (e.g., new products that customers want, new approaches to labor relations that help make a firm more competitive)

139

The Relationship of Change and Complexity to the Amount
of Leadership and Management Needed in a Firm

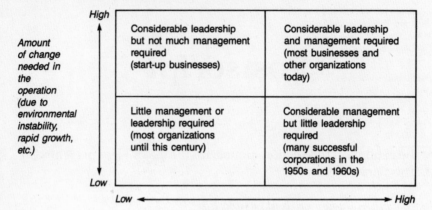

Consequences in the 1980s and 1990s of Strong Management with Weak Leadership

> A strong emphasis on short time frames, details, eliminating risks, and scrupulous rationality, with little focus on the long term, the big picture, strategies that take calculated risks, and people's values
>
> Plus a strong focus on specialization, fitting people to jobs, and compliance to rules, with little focus on integration, alignment, and commitment
>
> Plus a strong focus on containment, control, and predictability, with little emphasis on expansion, empowerment, and inspiration

↓

> A firm that is rigid, not innovative, and thus incapable of dealing with changes in its market, competitive, or technological environment; performance deteriorates slowly if the firm is in a strong market position, quickly if it is not

Consequences of Strong Leadership and Weak Management in a
Complex Organization

Strong long-term vision without short-term planning and budgeting, plus

An almost cult-like culture without much specialization, structures, and rules, plus

Inspired people who tend not to use control systems and problem-solving discipline

---

A situation that eventually gets out of control—critical deadlines, budgets, and promises are not met—threatening the very existence of the organization

How Executives in a Dozen Successful U.S. Firms Rate the People in Their Managerial Hierarchies

		Weak MANAGEMENT	Strong
LEADERSHIP	Strong	Nearly half say they have "too few"* people like this	Virtually all report "too few" people in this quadrant
	Weak	Half say they have "too many" people like this	Nearly two-thirds report "too many" people here

*Respondents were given three choices: (1) too few, (2) too many, (3) about right. The category having the largest number of responses is shown in the chart.

Creating an Agenda: Management vs. Leadership

	Management: Planning and Budgeting	Leadership: Establishing Direction
The primary function	To help produce predictable results on important dimensions (e.g., being on time and on budget) by planning for those results	To help produce changes needed to cope with a changing business environment (e.g., new products, new approaches to labor relations) by establishing a direction for change
A brief description of the activity	Developing a plan: a detailed map, put in written form if it is complicated and hard to remember or communicate, of how to achieve the results currently expected by important constituencies like customers and shareholders, along with timetables of what must be done when, by whom, and with the costs involved; doing so by means of a deductive process which starts with the needed results and then identifies the necessary steps, timetables, and costs	Developing direction: a vision which describes key aspects of an organization or activity in the future, along with a strategy for achieving that future state; doing so by means of an inductive process of gathering a broad range of information about the business, organization, or activity, answering basic questions about that domain, testing alternative directions against that understanding, possibly experimenting with some of the options, and then choosing one

The Interrelationship of Direction Setting and Planning in a Complex Organization

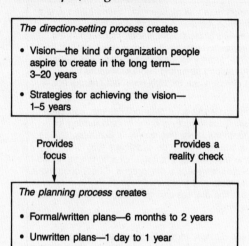

The direction-setting process creates

- Vision—the kind of organization people aspire to create in the long term— 3–20 years

- Strategies for achieving the vision— 1–5 years

Provides focus

Provides a reality check

The planning process creates

- Formal/written plans—6 months to 2 years

- Unwritten plans—1 day to 1 year

Establishing Direction

Direction	A description of something in the future (a vision), often the distant future, and a strategy for getting there. A good vision satisfies two tests: desirability and feasibility. Desirability means the needs of the constituencies that support the business or organization (e.g., customers, shareholders, employees) are met. Feasibility means there is a sensible strategy for getting there, one that takes into account the competition, the organization's strengths and weaknesses, technological trends, etc. A firm's direction can be very novel but often is not.
Creating direction	Gathering a broad range of information about an activity or business, especially from customers. Challenging conventional wisdom and analytically looking for patterns that answer very basic questions about that activity or business (e.g., what is required to succeed in the business? How do customers view our products/services?). Generating and then testing alternative directions against this understanding. Possibly even experimenting with some options. Finally choosing a good one (i.e., one that is both desirable and feasible). Doing all this in a dynamic way that never really ends (although the process can go through periods of great activity and periods of relative inactivity).
Potential impact	Clear direction helps produce useful change, especially significant or non-incremental change, by pointing out where a group should move, by showing how it can get there, and by providing a message that is potentially motivating/uplifting.

Developing a Human System/Network for Achieving Some Agenda:
Management vs. Leadership

	Management: Organizing & Staffing	Leadership: Aligning People
Primary function	Creating an organization that can implement plans, and thus help produce predictable results on important dimensions (e.g., costs, delivery schedules, product quality)	Getting people lined up behind a vision and set of strategies so as to help produce the change needed to cope with a changing environment (e.g., new products, new approaches to labor relations)
A brief description of the activity	A process of organizational design involving judgments about fit: what structure best fits the plan, what individual best fits each job in the structure, what part of the plan fits each person and thus should be delegated to him or her, what compensation system best fits the plan and the people involved, etc.	A major communications challenge: getting people to understand and believe the vision and strategies by communicating a great deal to all of the individuals whose cooperation or compliance may be needed to make that direction a reality, and doing so in as clear and credible a way as possible

Aligning People

Alignment	A condition in which a relevant group of people share a common understanding of a vision and set of strategies, accept the validity of that direction, and are willing to work toward making it a reality
Creating alignment	Communicating the direction as often as possible (repetition is important) to all those people (subordinates, subordinates of subordinates, bosses, suppliers, etc.) whose help or cooperation is needed; doing so, whenever possible, with simple images or symbols or metaphors that communicate powerfully without clogging already overused communications channels and without requiring a lot of scarce managerial time; making the message credible by using communicators with good track records and working relationships, by stating the message in as sensible a way as possible, by making sure the words and deeds of the communicators are consistent, and generally by demonstrating an unswerving dedication to the vision and strategies (so-called "leadership by example")
Potential impact	An aligned group of people has the potential of making progress toward some vision.

Execution: Management vs. Leadership

	Management: Controlling & Problem Solving	*Leadership:* Motivating & Inspiring
Function	To minimize deviations from plan, and thus help produce predictable results on important dimensions	To energize people to overcome major obstacles toward achieving a vision, and thus to help produce the change needed to cope with a changing environment
A brief description of the activity	Monitoring results versus plan in some detail, both formally and informally, by means of reports, meetings, and other control mechanisms, identifying deviations from plan, which are usually called "problems," and then planning and organizing to solve those problems	Satisfying very basic but often unfulfilled human needs—for achievement, belonging, recognition, self-esteem, a sense of control over one's life, living up to one's ideals—and thereby creating an unusually high energy level in people

Motivating and Inspiring

Motivated/ inspired people	A group of people who exhibit a level of energy, intensity, and determination far above what is considered normal. In a successful leadership effort this level of motivation tends to be sustained for relatively long periods of time.
Creating motivation and inspiration	Satisfying very basic human needs for achievement, belonging, recognition, self-esteem, a sense of control over one's life, living up to one's ideals, etc.; by 1) articulating again and again a vision in a way that stresses the key values of the people being communicated to, 2) involving those people in deciding how to achieve that vision or some portion of the vision, 3) supporting their efforts with coaching, feedback, role modeling, and a lot of of enthusiasm, and 4) sincerely recognizing in public and rewarding all of their successes.
Potential impact	A highly motivated group that is aligned to some direction can overcome major economic, bureaucratic, and political obstacles that stand in its way.

Management and Leadership Roles

	Management Roles	Leadership Roles
Purpose	To create management processes, and thus to help produce predictable results on important dimensions.	To create leadership processes, and thus to help produce changes needed to cope with a changing business environment.
Number	Usually 10-20% of the total jobs in an organization. In general, the more complex the operation, the more managerial roles.	Can vary enormously: 1–50% of the total jobs in an organization depending upon how much the operation needs to change.
Content	So called "line–management jobs" deal with all three aspects of management (planning, organizing, and control) for some domain. "Staff–management jobs" sometimes deal with only a limited piece of the overall process (e.g., budgeting or executive compensation) within some domain. Overall size of jobs can vary greatly from big to small.	Can vary enormously. Some will focus on all aspects of the leadership process for some activity or organization. Others will focus on a single aspect of the process (e.g., direction setting, or even one aspect of direction setting). Overall size of jobs can vary greatly from big (L) to small (l).
Assignment	Roles tend to be assigned to people as a formal part of the management process itself. People with management roles can also have leadership roles that are bigger or smaller than their management jobs.	Roles tend to be assigned or assumed by people in a more informal way and tend to be more fluid or changing. People with leadership roles usually also have management roles.

Coordinating Management Roles vs. Leadership Roles

	Multiple Management Roles	Multiple Leadership Roles
Primary coordinating mechanisms	Formal structure (job descriptions and chain of command) and integrated plans.	Thick informal networks (good working relationships among many people who share certain values) and overlapping visions.
Process by which mechanisms work	Job descriptions specify responsibilities and authority and reduce conflict by minimizing overlap between jobs. Chains of command link all jobs, and thus provide a vehicle for resolving conflict. These same mechanisms, when applied to the planning process, create an integrated set of plans, which eliminate future conflict.	The multitude of good communication channels and trust among people in thick informal networks allow for an ongoing process of accommodation and adaptation regarding who plays what role, and regarding conflict among roles. Those channels also help produce visions that are linked and compatible instead of remote and competitive.

Heredity, Childhood, and Leadership in Big Jobs

Traits From Heredity or Childhood	Effect on Leadership in Big Jobs
Drive/energy level	Without a great deal of inner drive, the difficulties in producing change over a period of years tend to discourage people from leading.
Intelligence/intellectual skills	Without sufficient basic intelligence, it is often difficult to set the right direction in a complex environment.
Mental/emotional health	Without some minimum amount of mental/emotional health, all the interpersonal skills needed for leadership tend not to develop over time. The distortions caused by emotional problems can also create tragically flawed visions.
Integrity	Large numbers of people never follow individuals who, they believe, to be lacking in integrity, except for short periods of time. Also, highly driven individuals who lack integrity often establish a course that, if people do follow, will eventually lead to tragedy.

Career Experiences and Leadership

	Career Experiences	Effect on Leadership
Promotes leadership	Challenging assignments early in a career	Stretches people, helping them to grow in many dimensions, some of which will be relevant to leadership; allows individuals to try leadership and learn from their successes and failures
	Visible leadership role models who are very good or very bad	Extreme examples, both good and bad, are easy to learn from, because the lessons are very clear
	Assignments which broaden	Breadth of knowledge is particularly important for direction setting, and breadth of contacts and relationships for alignment and motivation
Inhibits leadership	A long series of narrow and tactical jobs	Makes one short-term and tactically oriented; does not develop long-term and strategic skills
	Vertical career movement	Does not produce the breadth needed to lead in big jobs
	Rapid promotions	Does not help people to think long term or to learn the impact of their actions over the long term; can encourage a manipulative style
	Measurement and rewards based on short-term results only	Encourages people to pay attention to the management aspects of their jobs and ignore the leadership aspects; teaches management but not leadership

The Growth of Leadership and Management Capacity Over the Span of a Career

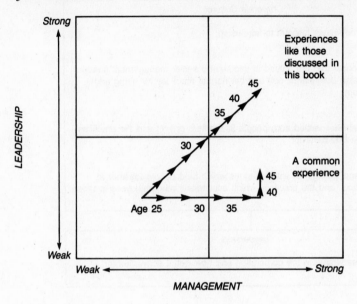

Corporate Culture and Leadership

> ### Corporate Culture
>
> Norms and shared values relevant to leadership:
>
> - The kind of people that are valued in middle and senior management (leaders or not, leadership potential or not) and the normal practices for hiring and developing them
>
> - The kind of behavior valued from people (leadership or not) and the practices that encourage that behavior
>
> - The number and strength of shared values which bind people together in informal networks, and the practices which acculturate new employees to those values

> ### Leadership
>
> The amount of leadership in the corporation and how well it converges (or conflicts)

APPENDIX

The Research

About halfway through the research that led to my last book, *The Leadership Factor*, I became convinced that the differences between management and leadership were both important and poorly understood. To pursue this line of thought in more depth, I designed a two-part study (see Exhibit I) that has culminated in this book.

The first phase of this research involved the creation of the questionnaire shown in Exhibit II. That survey was eventually administered to a total of 200 senior executives, business people who were working for twelve highly successful U.S. corporations. In about one-third of the cases, the questionnaire was administered in a one-hour interview. In the rest of the cases, it was mailed to the executives and filled out by them alone.

The second phase of this research first involved the location of a dozen cases of "highly effective leadership in business." (See Exhibit III for the solicitation letter.) I then documented each of these cases, mostly through interviews (see Exhibit IV).

Exhibit I *The Study*

1. Initial design of the research	June 1986–August 1986
2. Creation of the questionnaire	August 1986–November 1986
3. Securing the cooperation of 200 executives to answer the questionnaire	October 1986–May 1987
4. Administration of the questionnaire	January 1987–June 1987
5. Analysis of questionnaire data	May 1987–December 1987
6. Locating "Effective Leadership" stories and gaining the cooperation of the people involved	June 1987–September 1988
7. Interviewing people to document the stories	August 1987–October 1988
8. Analyzing the stories and writing them up	June 1988–December 1988
9. Preparing this manuscript	September 1988–October 1989

Exhibit II *The Questionnaire*

I. Please list below the initials of a fairly random sample of ten people with whom you work by doing the following: Think of bosses, colleagues, subordinates, or even others outside your firm (with whom you work) who have last names that start with the same last letter as your last name. Write their initials below, then go to the next letter in the alphabet and do the same, continuing until you have ten sets of initials (e.g., Kotter. I have worked recently with Fred Kolb, Joe Kennedy, John Lintman, Jim Leahey, Jeff Lynn, Paul Lawrence, Jay Lorsch, John McArthur, Warren McFarlan, and Fred Mallot. So I would write in the space below: FK, JK, JLi, JLeh, JLy, PL, JLo, JM, WM, FM).

1) _____ 2) _____ 3) _____ 4) _____ 5) _____

6) _____ 7) _____ 8) _____ 9) _____ 10) _____

II. Please evaluate how much each of these ten people contributes to the management of the people and activities around him or her: 6 = very strong contribution to the management process, 5 = strong contribution, 4 = contribution, 3 = weak contribution, 2 = very weak contribution, 1 = no contribution.

Person 1 ____ Person 2 ____ Person 3 ____ Person 4 ____

Person 5 ____ Person 6 ____ Person 7 ____ Person 8 ____

Person 9 ____ Person 10 ____

III. Now please evaluate how much each of these ten people contributes to the leadership of the people and activities around him or her. Again, 6 = very strong contributor to the leadership process, etc.

Person 1 ____ Person 2 ____ Person 3 ____ Person 4 ____

Person 5 ____ Person 6 ____ Person 7 ____ Person 8 ____

Person 9 ____ Person 10 ____

IV. Now think of someone you know personally (it does not have to be one of the ten people listed previously) who you think has done an outstanding job of effectively managing the people and activities around him or her, and describe below, in as much detail as possible, exactly what he or she has done that constitutes this extremely effective management.

He or she _____

_____

_____

He or she _____

_____

_____

He or she _____

_____

_____

He or she _____

_____

_____

He or she _____

_____

_____

He or she _____

_____

_____

He or she _____

_____

_____

He or she _____

_____

_____

He or she _____

_____

_____

He or she _____

_____

_____

V. Now think of someone you know personally who in your judg-
    ment has done an outstanding job of providing effective leader-
    ship to the people and activities around him or her, and then
    describe, in as much detail as possible, exactly what he or she
    has done that constitutes "highly effective leadership."

He or she _____
_____
_____

He or she _____
_____
_____

He or she _____
_____
_____

He or she _____
_____
_____

He or she _____
_____
_____

He or she _____
_____
_____

He or she _____
_____
_____

He or she _____
_____
_____

He or she _____
_____
_____

He or she _____
_____
_____

VI.   Now, look at the figure below and think of *all* of the people who are in management jobs in your corporation.

		Weak	Strong
LEADERSHIP	Strong	2	3
	Weak	1	4

Weak   Strong

MANAGEMENT

For your corporation to continue to be successful over the next ten years, do you have the right number of people in each of the four quadrants in the figure shown above? Or, are there too few people in some quadrants? Or are there too many in some?

Quadrant #1: the right # _____, too few _____, too many _____?

Quadrant #2: the right # _____, too few _____, too many _____?

Quadrant #3: the right # _____, too few _____, too many _____?

Quadrant #4: the right # _____, too few _____, too many _____?

Exhibit III *Solicitation Letter*

Dear

As a part of my ongoing research on the subject of managerial behavior, I am in the process of looking for situations that exemplify extraordinarily effective leadership. I do not much care if the story involves a CEO or a foreman, one person or thousands, a time period of three months or ten years. The only thing that is important is that well-informed parties agree a central element in the situation is "highly effective leadership."

If you can think of a case that fits this specification, and would be willing to help me obtain interviews with the people involved so as to document that story, I would greatly appreciate hearing from you. My telephone number is (617) 495-6529, and I can be reached by mail at the Harvard Business School, Boston, MA 02163.

Thank you very much for considering this request.

With best regards,

John P. Kotter

Exhibit IV *Interview Guide for Leadership Stories*

1. (Background on interviewee) First, if you would tell me a little about yourself. You have worked for this firm how long? (Probe to get a summary of his/her career.)

2. Tell me about _____ (the story being documented). Perhaps if you would start at the beginning and then describe the major events. (Probe for as much detail as possible; *Who* did *what, when, how,* and *why?*)

3. (If other interviews have left some points confusing or provided contradictory information, raise specific questions here to resolve those issues.)

4. Results from this episode—how important are they to the corporation? Why do you say this? (Probe both for specific results and find out why the interviewee thinks they are important or unimportant.)

5. How large a role did "effective leadership" play in this story? If interviewee feels effective leadership was central to the story ask: Who helped provide the leadership? What exactly did they do that constituted effective leadership?

6. If a small number of people were the principal suppliers of leadership, say: Tell me about each of these people. Why were they able to provide effective leadership?

Notes

Preface

1. Kotter and Lawrence, *Mayors in Action: Five Approaches to Urban Governance*, John Wiley, 1974.

2. Kotter, *Organizational Dynamics: Diagnosis and Intervention*, Addison-Wesley, 1978.

3. Kotter, Faux, and McArthur, *Self-Assessment and Career Development*, Prentice-Hall, 1978.

4. Kotter, Schlesinger, and Sathe, *Organization: Text, Cases and Readings on the Management of Organization Design and Change*, Richard D. Irwin, 1979.

5. Kotter, *Power in Management*, AMACOM, 1979; and *Power and Influence: Beyond Formal Authority*, Free Press, 1985.

6. Kotter, *The General Managers*, Free Press, 1982.

7. Kotter, *The Leadership Factor*, Free Press, 1988.

8. Comparative analysis requires cases of both success and failure. I did not gather negative examples here because my earlier studies have identified many instances of ineffective leadership.

CHAPTER 1 Management and Leadership

1. A sizable amount of the literature on leadership is based on studies of people in supervisory or managerial jobs, people who may or may not have been providing effective leadership. See Bass (*Handbook of Leadership: A Survey of Theory and Research*, Free Press, 1981) and Yukl (*Leadership in Organizations*, Prentice-Hall, 1989).

2. This is not to suggest that management, at least in an elementary form, did not exist centuries earlier. It surely did, and generals, kings, and high priests undoubtedly knew something about it. But the management they knew and used was the product of a vastly less complicated age. Compared to today, the organizations they managed were technologically simple and usually small—in other words, not very complex.

3. Chandler, *The Visible Hand,* Belknap Press of Harvard University Press, 1977.

4. Summarized here are the elements of management most commonly included in both a) the many books on that subject published in this century, and b) a 1987 survey conducted by this author which asked 200 executives to describe the actions of someone they knew who was effectively managing whatever he or she was responsible for.

5. Although not the only function, that seems to be the most common one mentioned in the hundreds of books on management that have been published in the past 60 to 70 years.

6. Burns, *Leadership,* Harper & Row, 1978.

7. Levinson and Rosenthal end their study of CEO's with the following conclusion; "Strong leaders are necessary, particularly for organizations that must undergo significant change. Not good managers or executives, but strong leaders." (*CEO: Corporate Leadership in Action,* Basic Books, 1984, p. 289.)

8. Determining what "generally better off" and "trampling on the rights of others" mean, in practice, can be most difficult and has led to endless philosophical discussions. For the purposes of this book, effectiveness is measured by the cumulative after-the-fact opinions of all those affected by a leadership process.

9. The list is generally consistent with other important works on leadership in modern organizations—books by Bennis and Nanus (*Leaders: The Strategies for Taking Charge,* Harper & Row, 1985) and Peters and Austin (*A Passion for Excellence: The Leadership Difference,* Random House, 1985), for example. But this specific way of thinking about leadership comes from the studies upon which the book is based (see the Preface).

10. The distinction between leadership and management is similar in some ways to what Burns (*op. cit.*) and Bass (*Leadership and Performance Beyond Expectations,* Free Press, 1985) have called transformational leadership versus transactional leadership. The book by Burns and a 1977 article by Zaleznik ("Managers and Leaders: Are They Different", *Harvard Business Review, 55,* 5, pp. 67–87) are the first two works of which I am aware that begin to explore these differences.

11. For a fascinating analysis of the pure types and their potential for conflict, see Zaleznik, *op. cit.*, pp. 67–80.

12. This occurred in China during the "Cultural Revolution."

13. Very visible examples, although not extreme ones, include Apple before John Sculley became CEO and People Express during its final year of operation.

14. Approximately 200 executives were polled during 1987 either with a questionnaire or in an hour-long interview (see Appendix). The dimensions of "management" and "leadership" were not defined for them, but before they were asked to rate their fellow managers on those dimensions, they were first asked to describe in detail the actions of someone they knew who provided effective management and then to describe likewise the actions of someone who has provided effective leadership.

15. Further details on this survey can be found in Kotter, *The Leadership Factor*, Free Press, 1988.

16. *Ibid.* Chapter 6.

17. By "entrepreneurial" I mean leaders who focused their energies on taking advantage of opportunities to build businesses.

18. The sheer amount of management education offered today is at least thirty times greater than that offered fifty years ago.

19. Kotter, *op. cit.*, Chapter 3.

20. Beckhard, *Organizational Development*, Addison-Wesley, 1969.

CHAPTER 2 Leadership in Action

1. Information in this chapter comes from NCR company documents plus interviews with Jim Adamson, Bill Bird, Darrell Clark, Ed Connal, Robert Corcos, Kurt Hanaway, Fred Hutcheon, Ken Kelly, Grant Keir, Charlie Loarridge, Alan Murdoch, Bill Patullo, M.Y. (Joe) Stephan, John Tosh, and Nigel Vincent.

2. All twelve of the case studies done in conjunction with the research for this book contain these themes.

3. All twelve of the in-depth case studies that were researched for this book have fairly dramatic results. Furthermore, the stories of "effective leadership," reported in the 200 interviews or questionnaires that were also a part of this research, almost all show similar results.

CHAPTER 3 Establishing Direction

1. This example is planning in its simplest form. In many real situations, deductions will be much more complex. Furthermore, the planning

process will often go through two or more iterations before a plan is produced that fits all constraints, such as those set by still other plans.

2. The concept of vision, used in this context, was first convincingly demonstrated by leadership studies conducted by Tichy and Bennis. See Tichy and Devanna (*The Transformational Leader*, Wiley, 1986) and Bennis and Nanus (*Leaders: The Strategies for Taking Charge*, Harper & Row, 1985).

3. Pascale and Athos call vision "superordinate goals" and argue that such goals should be 1) significant (desirable), 2) durable (long term), and 3) achievable (feasible). See their discussion in *The Art of Japanese Management*, Simon & Schuster, 1981.

4. Information on TRS comes from company documents, interviews with executives (Ed Cooperman, Lou Gerstner, Ron Glover, David Kalis, Jonathan Linen, Phillip Riese, and Rick Thoman), and informal discussions with a dozen middle-level American Express employees.

5. "The Hazards Down the Track for American Express," *Fortune,* Nov. 6, 1978, p. 106.

6. Information on SAS comes from Carlzon's book, *Moments of Truth* (Ballinger Publishing, 1987), company documents, and an interview with Mr. Carlzon.

7. ICI's profitability rose at nearly 40 percent per year compounded when Harvey-Jones was chairman.

8. Harvey-Jones, *Making It Happen: Reflections on Leadership*, Collins, 1988, p. 25.

CHAPTER 4 Aligning People

1. Pioneering work has been done by people such as Lawrence and Lorsch (*Organization and Environment*, Harvard Business School Press, 1967) at Harvard. See also Nystrom and Starbuck, *Handbook of Organizational Design,* Oxford University Press, 1981.

2. For a discussion of the importance of lateral relationships in the production of innovative change, see Kanter ("The Middle Manager as Innovator," *Harvard Business Review,* July-August, 1982; and *The Change Masters,* Simon & Schuster, 1983).

3. A 1987 speech to the Society of Automotive Engineers.

4. There are a number of classic examples of this problem in Kotter, *Power and Influence,* Free Press, 1985, Part II.

5. Information about Kodak comes from internal company documents plus interviews with Martin Berwick, John Bricklemyer, Robet Crandall, Richard Hamer, Alan Lefko, Richard Psyk, Thomas Roztocil, Wilfrid Rowe, and Joseph Schliff.

6. Leaders empower people through alignment and, as described in Chapter 5, their approach to motivation.

CHAPTER 5 Motivating and Inspiring

1. The term *homeostasis* was invented for a different purpose, but hopefully its originator would not be offended by the usage here. See Cannon, *The Wisdom of the Body* (rev. ed.), Norton, 1939.

2. Hackman and Oldman ("Motivation Through the Design of Work: Test of a Theory," *Organizational Behavior and Human Performance, 16,* 1976; and *Work Redesign,* Addison-Wesley, 1980), and Aldaq and Brief (*Task Design and Employee Motivation,* Scott, Foresman, 1979).

3. The word *inspire* is used here to mean a form of motivation which appeals to ideals.

4. Information about Mary Kay comes from interviews conducted for a 1981 Harvard Business School case, and from public source material.

5. Beauty consultants and sales directors are not Mary Kay employees but independent business agents.

6. This was reported in the press in 1985 and is still believed to be true as of this writing in 1989.

7. The first Wal-Mart store was opened in 1962.

8. Information about Kentucky Fried Chicken comes from company documents and interviews with Phil Bouckaert, Don Doyle, Ed Dudley, Bill Evans, Roger Kramer, Ottie Ladd, Dick Mayer, Shelby Massey, Gregg Reynolds, Dr. G. V. Rao, and Harry Sunenshine.

9. Mike Miles left KFC in 1982. In 1989, as CEO at Kraft General Foods, he convinced Dick Mayer to once again team up with him. Dick is now president of General Foods.

CHAPTER 6 Multiple Roles

1. See the recent discussion and examples by Barnes and Kriger, "The Hidden Side of Organizational Leadership," *Sloan Management Review,* Fall 1986, pp. 15–25.

2. Information regarding ARCO comes from company documents plus interviews with Ron Arnault, George Babikian, Lod Cook, Jim Morrison, Don Murray, Scott Stamworth, and Bob Wycoff.

3. November 7, 1988.

4. *Forbes,* March 21, 1988.

5. *Ibid.*

6. ARCO's ROE was 25.9%, and second–place Exxon's was 16.8% (as reported in *Business Week*).

7. As of this writing Anderson is, once again, an oil entrepreneur, running a small firm.

8. These figures depend on whether the difference is measured by revenues, assets, or number of people involved.

9. Kotter, *The Leadership Factor,* Free Press, 1988.

10. Information on Decworld '87 comes from internal company documents and interviews with Kerry Bensman, Carmen Coletta, Dallas Kirk, Janet Shipman, Elizabeth Strong, Barbara Wood, and Craig Zamzow.

CHAPTER 7   **Thick Informal Networks**

1. For a broader discussion of all this, see Kotter, Schlesinger, and Sathe (*Organization,* Richard D. Irwin, 1979) and Galbraith (*Organization Design,* Addison-Wesley, 1977).

2. *Ibid.*

3. Eccles and Crane, *Doing Deals,* Harvard Business School Press, 1988.

4. Information on P&G comes from company documents, plus interviews with nine P&G managers who were centrally involved in the effort described here.

5. *Wall St. Journal,* August 9, 1989, p. 1, second section.

6. All names except for Nicolosi's have been disguised at P&G's request.

CHAPTER 8   **Heredity and Childhood**

1. Kotter, *The General Managers,* Free Press, 1982.

2. Mintzberg (*The Nature of Managerial Work,* Harper & Row, 1973; and "The Manager's Job: Folklore and Fact," *Harvard Business Review,* July-August, 1975) and Stewart (*Managers and Their Jobs,* Macmillan, 1967; *Contrasts in Management,* McGraw-Hill UK, 1976; and *Choices for the Manager: A Guide to Understanding Managerial Work,* Prentice-Hall, 1982).

3. Kotter, *op. cit.,* Chapter 2.

4. Psychologist David McClelland has called this "power and achievement motivation" and has argued, successfully, that it is commonly found among successful executives. See McClelland (*Power: The Inner Experience,* Irvington, 1975) and McClelland and Boyatzis ("Leadership Motive Pattern and Long–term Success in Management," *Journal of Applied Psychology, 67,* 1982).

5. Iacocca, *Iacocca: An Autobiography,* Bantam Books, 1984.

6. See Boyatzis' discussion of cognitive skills in *The Competent Manager,* Wiley, 1982.

7. Hogan, Raskin, and Fazzini, "The Dark Side of Charisma," Working Paper, Tulsa Institute of Behavioral Sciences, 1989.

8. Boyatzis, *op. cit.*

9. For example, if one in ten has the drive, one in three has the intelligence, one in two has the mental health, and one in two has the integrity, and if these elements are relatively independent (they may not be), then one in 120 will have all four ($\frac{1}{10} \times \frac{1}{3} \times \frac{1}{2} \times \frac{1}{2} = \frac{1}{120}$).

10. Kotter, *The Leadership Factor,* Free Press, 1988, Chapter 7.

11. An interesting exception can be seen in the case of some of Japan's best companies. They have not stressed technical qualifications in most entry-level hiring but more general traits like intelligence and interpersonal skills.

CHAPTER 9 Career Experiences

1. McCall, Lombardo, and Morrison, *The Lessons of Experience,* Lexington Books, 1988; and Kotter, *The General Managers,* Free Press, 1982.

2. Harvey-Jones, *Making It Happen: Reflections on Leadership,* Collins, 1988, p. 61.

3. McCall, Lombardo, and Morrison, *op. cit.*

4. Ash, *Mary Kay on People Management,* Warner Books, 1984, pp. 4–5.

5. See my discussion of how career experiences empower, Kotter, *Power and Influence,* Free Press, 1985, Chapter 7.

6. Information about Enrico comes from an interview with him, supplemented by interviews with a few of his colleagues at Pepsi.

7. For a broad discussion of these issues and a presentation of the evidence supporting this conclusion, see Kotter, *The Leadership Factor,* Part II.

8. *Ibid.,* Chapter 7.

CHAPER 10 Corporate Culture

1. In a 1988 survey conducted by Harvard Professor James Heskett and myself, these firms were rated by executives in their industries as having strong corporate cultures.

2. Kotter, *op. cit.,* pp. 98–99.

3. Information on ConAgra comes from company documents plus interviews with Bob Daugherty, Paul Graven, Mike Harper, Jim Kennedy,

Andy Langert, Bud Morrison, Gilbert Mulhere, David Pederson, Scott Rahn, Don Rasche, Jerry Vernon, and Bob White.

4. Professor James Heskett and I polled over sixty senior executives in the food industry with a short questionnaire. Approximately half responded.

5. In terms of 1987 revenues, Philip Morris/Kraft, Unilever, Nestle, Procter & Gamble, RJR Nabisco, B.A.T. Industries, PepsiCo, and Sara Lee were larger.

6. As this is being written, despite the power and success of ConAgra's culture, it is not clear how well it has been institutionalized, and thus exists independent of Mike Harper. This will only become known after he retires. The same can also be said, at least to some degree, for the cultures developed by all the other individuals discussed in previous chapters.

7. Schein, *Organizational Culture and Leadership,* Jossey-Bass, 1985.

Bibliography

ALDAQ, R. J., and BRIEF, A. P. *Task Design and Employee Motivation*. Glenview, IL: Scott, Foresman, 1979.

ASH, M. K. *Mary Kay on People Management*. New York: Warner Books, 1984.

BARNES, L. B., and KRIGER, M. P. "The Hidden Side of Organizational Leadership." *Sloan Management Review* (Fall 1986), pp. 15–25.

BASS, B. M. *Handbook of Leadership: A Survey of Theory and Research*. New York: Free Press, 1981.

BASS, B. M. *Leadership and Performance Beyond Expectations*. New York: Free Press, 1985.

BECKHARD, R. *Organizational Development*. Reading, MA: Addison-Wesley, 1969.

BENNIS, W. G., and NANUS, B. *Leaders: The Strategies for Taking Charge*. New York: Harper & Row, 1985.

BOYATZIS, R. E. *The Competent Manager*. New York: John Wiley, 1982.

BURNS, J. M. *Leadership*. New York: Harper & Row, 1978.

CANNON, W. B. *The Wisdom of the Body*. New York: Norton (rev. ed.), 1939.

CARLZON, J. *Moments of Truth*. Cambridge, MA: Ballinger Publishing, 1987.

CHANDLER, A. *The Visible Hand*. Cambridge, MA: Belknap Press of Harvard University Press, 1977.

ECCLES, R. G., and CRANE, D. B. *Doing Deals*. Boston: Harvard Business School Press, 1988.

GALBRAITH, J. R. *Organization Design*. Reading, MA: Addison-Wesley, 1977.

HACKMAN, J. R., and OLDHAM, G. R. "Motivation Through the Design of Work:

Test of a Theory." *Organizational Behavior and Human Performance, 16* (1976), pp. 250–279.

HACKMAN, J. R., and OLDHAM, G. R. *Work Redesign.* Reading, MA: Addison-Wesley, 1980.

HARVEY-JONES, J. *Making It Happen: Reflections on Leadership.* London: Collins, 1988.

HOGAN, R., RASKIN, R., and FAZZINI, D. "The Dark Side of Charisma." Working Paper, Tulsa Institute of Behavioral Sciences, 1989.

IACOCCA, L., with NOVAK, W. *Iacocca: An Autobiography.* New York: Bantam Books, 1984.

KANTER, R. M. "The Middle Manager as Innovator." *Harvard Business Review* (July–August 1982), pp. 95–105.

KANTER, R. M. *The Change Masters.* New York: Simon & Schuster, 1983.

KOTTER, J. P. *Organizational Dynamics: Diagnosis and Intervention.* Reading, MA: Addison-Wesley, 1978.

KOTTER, J. P. *Power in Management.* New York: AMACOM, 1979.

KOTTER, J. P. *The General Managers.* New York: Free Press, 1982.

KOTTER, J. P. *Power and Influence: Beyond Formal Authority.* New York: Free Press, 1985.

KOTTER, J. P. *The Leadership Factor.* New York: Free Press, 1988.

KOTTER, J. P., and LAWRENCE, P. R. *Mayors in Action: Five Approaches in Urban Governance.* New York: John Wiley, 1974.

KOTTER, J. P. with FAUX, V. and McARTHUR, C. *Self-Assessment and Career Development.* Englewood Cliffs, NJ: Prentice-Hall, 1978.

KOTTER, J. P., SCHLESINGER, L., and SATHE, V. J. *Organization: Text, Cases and Readings on the Management of Organization Design and Change.* Homewood, IL: Richard D. Irwin, 1979.

LAWRENCE, P. R., & LORSCH, J. W. *Organization and Environment.* Boston: Harvard Business School Press, 1967.

LEVINSON, H., and ROSENTHAL, S. *CEO: Corporate Leadership in Action.* New York: Basic Books, 1984.

McCALL, M. W., LOMBARDO, M. M. and MORRISON, A. M. *The Lessons of Experience.* Lexington, MA: Lexington Books, 1988.

McCLELLAND, D. C. *Power: The Inner Experience.* New York: Irvington, 1975.

McCLELLAND, D. C., and BOYATZIS, R. E. "Leadership Motive Pattern and Long Term Success in Management." *Journal of Applied Psychology, 67* (1982), pp. 737–743.

MINTZBERG, H. *The Nature of Managerial Work.* New York: Harper & Row, 1973.

MINTZBERG, H. "The Manager's Job: Folklore and Fact." *Harvard Business Review* (July–August 1975), pp. 49–61.

NYSTROM, P. C., and STARBUCK, W. H. *Handbook of Organizational Design.* Oxford/New York: Oxford University Press, 1981.

PASCALE, R. T., and ATHOS, A. G. *The Art of Japanese Management.* New York: Simon & Schuster, 1981.

PETERS, T. J., and AUSTIN, N. *A Passion for Excellence: The Leadership Difference.* New York: Random House, 1985.

SCHEIN, E. H. *Organizational Culture and Leadership.* San Francisco: Jossey-Bass, 1985.

STEWART, R. *Managers and Their Jobs.* London: Macmillan, 1967.

STEWART, R. *Contrasts in Management.* Maidenhead, Berkshire, England: McGraw-Hill UK, 1976.

STEWART, R. *Choices for the Manager: A Guide to Understanding Managerial Work.* Englewood Cliffs, NJ: Prentice-Hall, 1982.

TICHY, N. M. & DEVANNA, M. A. *The Transformational Leader.* New York: John Wiley, 1986.

YUKL, G. A. *Leadership in Organizations.* 2nd ed. Englewood Cliffs, NJ: Prentice-Hall, 1989.

ZALEZNIK, A. "Managers and Leaders: Are They Different?" *Harvard Business Review, 55* (5) (1977), pp. 67–78.

Index